Crea

God's Steward

[handwritten inscription: To Howard: My good friend and excellent teacher. ISAIAH 64:8]

Copyright February 11, 2020 by George C. Hale

ISBN: 9781696258333

Cover design: Splash Box Marketing, LLC www.splashbox.com

Editing: Julianna Hale www. juliannahale.com

All Scripture quotations are from the New King James Version unless noted otherwise.

CREATED FOR A PURPOSE

ACKNOWLEDGEMENTS

The Senior Pastor of Mariners Church, Irvine California in 2005, Kenton Beshore, required every leader to work with a team on every act of ministry. There were no exceptions. Kenton was brilliant when it came to leading a church. He led the growth of Mariners Church from a beginning attendance of around one hundred fifty worshipers to an attendance that exceeded twenty thousand adults on many weekends.

Kenton put together a team to develop a white paper on "The Philosophy and Practice of Stewardship" at Mariners Church. I kicked the project off with my lengthy paper on the subject of stewardship, which I had developed many years earlier. However, it still took the team almost a year to craft the finished paper, which was later adopted by the Mariners' Elder Board.

Each team member added to the white paper. Evidence of their input is reflected in this book, so I want to acknowledge their meaningful contributions. The team was led by Paul Neff, a longtime member of Mariners, who served as the volunteer Chief Financial Officer until the church could afford to hire a full-time CFO. Paul is full of wisdom and love for God, and his life models being God's steward. He led the team well. In addition to Paul and myself, the other team members were Jeremey Moser, Susan Griffiths, and Bruce Nelson.

Paul funded a foundation, Servant's Heart Ministry, and spends much of his time managing that foundation; Jeremey became the CFO for Mariners Church after I left the position; and Bruce became the first Pastor of Stewardship for Mariners Church. Susan got married and Pastor Kenton retired.

Stewardship encompasses all that I do after I first accept Jesus Christ as my Lord and Savior. And to properly understand stewardship is to grasp the very essence of worshiping, serving and pleasing God. Once you grab hold of it your whole life will change, beginning with your heart. You will become a joyous giver of your time, your talent and yes, your treasure. You will become God's Steward, which is why God created you.

PREFACE

While serving as the executive pastor and chief financial officer of Mariners Church (Irvine, CA), I had the privilege of developing, with a team of volunteers, and implementing a written policy on biblical stewardship. This comprehensive plan was designed by our team to set forth biblically based guiding values in the areas of financial philosophy and ministry approach to stewardship.

The results were astonishing! The first year after Mariners Church leadership implemented this plan, general fund contributions rose from ten and a half million dollars to twenty million dollars annually. The church continued to experience financial growth, as general revenues soon hit the forty million dollar mark and has remained at that mark. During this same period of general fund growth, attendance remained steady at around twenty thousand attendees, and Mariners Church also raised almost one hundred million dollars to further develop the campus.

As impressive as they are, the dollar figures are not the main point. I share them only as a testimony to illustrate what I believe was God's blessing on Mariners Church for intentionally aligning stewardship practices to principles written in His Word.

After all, giving is not God's plan for raising money for the church—giving is God's plan to raise disciples of Jesus Christ. Our motive as leaders should not be to collect money but to witness the blessings bestowed to people when they live lives as generous givers to God's kingdom.

The financial result is only one part of the Mariners Church story. People volunteered their time and talent in unprecedented ways and amounts. Why? Because God captured their hearts.

This happened as a result of Mariners' leadership teaching Biblically based principles regarding stewardship. When God's truth is put into practice the result is profound.

During Mariners' capital campaign to fund the campus build out, a young man came by my office to see me. Ray (let's call him that) had just sold his business for around $1.2 billion dollars. As we talked, he slid a check over to me and said it was for the capital campaign.

I looked at the amount ... one million dollars. After considering this for a moment I slid the check back to Ray and I said, "Ray, this just does not seem like the correct amount to me. Have you prayed about your gift?" Ray looked a bit shocked and he finally said "No, not really."

We talked about Biblical stewardship for a while and at the end of our conversation I told him that God wanted his heart, not his million dollars. I asked him to pray over the gift with his wife and then decide whether to give, and how much to give to the Church. But I said that the important consideration was giving his heart to God, and that meant committing everything to God.

Weeks later I was told that Ray had made a large contribution to the building project. I never checked to find out how much, but a little latter Ray again came by to talk. He said he had purchased a new home and, after praying about it, he would like to donate his old house to Mariners. That house easily sold for just over three million dollars for Mariners Church.

Later, when the capital campaign had ended, I arranged for Mariners to borrow around twenty-five million dollars to complete the construction. This loan was paid off by a single donor. Was Ray the donor? I simply do not know, as I had left Mariners Church by then to partner with Pastor David Jeremiah at Turning Point for God Ministries. But, I do know that God changes people one heart at a time.

The doctrine of stewardship in the Christian community traces its origin to the book of Genesis in the Bible and is woven throughout God's Word. It brushes upon every nuance of life, impacts every decision and affects all that God places in our lives. It is not about money... it is about the heart of a believer.

Stewardship encompasses all that I do after I first accept Jesus Christ as my Lord and Savior. And to properly understand stewardship is to grasp the very essence of worshiping, serving and pleasing God. Once you grab hold of it your whole life will change, beginning with your heart. You will become a joyous giver of your time, your talent and yes, your treasure. You will become God's Steward, which is why God created you.

"Worship is giving God the best that He has given you. Be careful what you do with the best you have. Whenever you get a blessing from God, give it back to Him as a love gift. Take time to meditate before God and offer the blessing back to Him in a deliberate act of worship. If you hoard a thing for yourself, it will turn into spiritual dry rot, as the manna did when it was hoarded. God will never let you hold a spiritual thing for yourself; it has to be given back to Him that He may make it a blessing to others." Oswald Chambers

INTRODUCTION

Barbara James, a 62-year-old grandmother and a committed Christian, had been on the donor list waiting to receive a heart for several years. She struggled daily to stay alive and to keep her hopes up. She became a prayer warrior. However, as the weeks and months crept past, her situation was becoming dire. The doctors became more concerned, as did Barbara's family.

Then, a hospital in Atlanta, Georgia contacted Barbara—they had a viable heart for her that was a good match. Barbara was driven the 180 miles, accompanied by her husband and oldest child, to the hospital. There was much rejoicing among the James family as Barbara was being prepared for the surgery.

While this was taking place, the case of Heather Matthews, a 19-year-old who also needed a heart, became much more urgent. Without a transplant, doctors feared Heather had perhaps only days to live.

Heather's doctors determined that the heart slated for Barbara James was also a match for Heather. These doctors went to Barbara, who was at the same hospital, and asked her if she would agree to give up her opportunity, so that Heather would be the one to receive the available heart.

Barbara said "Yes".

Heather received the heart and is doing well, whereas Barbara was placed back at the top of the heart donor list. She passed away quietly in her sleep six months later, before another acceptable heart could be located.

In her humble Columbus, Georgia home, surrounded by family, just before going to be with Jesus, Barbara shared that she had done the right thing by allowing the available heart to go to the young woman. She told the family that she could not have lived with herself if she had chosen to receive the heart and Heather had died.

Money, and other possessions, such as the right to receive a heart transplant, have the potential of being a great blessing to others or they can become a life impacting negative influence.

Some, like Barbara James get it, whereas others like the Rich Young Ruler, written about by Luke (Luke 18: 18-23), will miss Jesus completely as they choose their possessions over Yeshua. Other believers will suffer the consequences of living with a conflicted heart while trying to balance loyalties to both God and possessions.

Biblical stewardship teaching, dedicated to developing the heart of a believer, and growing disciples of Jesus Christ is necessary for every believer, and for every Church and Christian Ministry.

Without addressing stewardship intentionally with effective biblical teaching and leadership, Ministries and Churches run the risk of God's people losing their way in the affluence of culture. The church today faces the same risks and challenges spoken about to the church in Laodicea in Revelation chapter 3.

Along with affluence comes the very real possibility that people will not see their need for God, but rather will join those whom Jesus charged as lukewarm and ultimately not worthy of fellowship with Him.

> "I know all the things you do, that you are neither hot nor cold. I wish you were one or the other! But since you are like lukewarm water, I will spit you out of my mouth!

You say, 'I am rich. I have everything I want. I don't need a thing!' And you don't realize that you are wretched and miserable and poor and blind and naked." Revelations 3:15-17

To assist the Christian believer as he or she seeks to know the purpose of their lives, and to help the Christian community as it seeks to develop fully devoted followers of Jesus Christ, I have written, over the past forty years, this book. It is intended to set forth biblically based guiding principles and precepts of stewardship.

With all of the books written about stewardship and about the purpose of one's life, why one more? Two reasons: one is the fact of an inescapable leading of the Holy Spirit to write such a book, which has pressed against my soul for four decades, and two is my belief that much of what I have written and what you are about to read, has never been put into a book. At least, I have not encountered such a book.

Although I have been educated at a Southern Baptist Seminary, and have served as the executive pastor for two of the largest protestant churches in the United States, I am actually a Certified Public Accountant and a banker by education, training and practice. A numbers person, grounded in the logical and practical things of life. There is just not much grey area in life for me.

Therefore, what I present in this book is from the standpoint of where the rubber hits the road. How do we achieve God's purpose, live out stewardship and our Christian witness, in the everyday stuff of life?

This is a book filled with scripture, because in the end, we should want to know what God has written about our purpose, and not what I, nor anyone else has to write.

Please, do not skip past the scripture.

The key to a life of purpose is the Word of God where He has revealed to us His truth. I have learned that God's Word tells the true story of stewardship and that I am but a humble tour guide shinning a spotlight on the truth of His Word.

Often we treat God's Word as a collection of disconnected gems of wisdom. I confess that I have done this. However, in doing this, we lose sight of God's written development of His redemptive purposes through His progressive revealing of Himself. When we view God's Word in its proper way, understanding of our purpose becomes abundantly clear.

In an attempt to illuminate God's Word regarding our purpose and stewardship, my desire was to tell the Mariners Church story, part of my journey, and some of the stories of others, in such a way as to weave them into a tapestry together with His Word, that would honor God and share His story.

My prayer is that hearts will be transformed into the image of Christ. May God richly bless you as you ponder His words regarding your purpose in life of becoming "God's Steward".

"All Christians are but God's stewards. Everything we have is on loan from the Lord, entrusted to us for a while to use in serving Him." – John MacArthur

MISSION

Unless it's your last day to live on earth, every person is given the same amount of time each day ... twenty four hours. When I was a paperboy in Columbus, Georgia I had the same amount of time each day as when I was a Bank CEO in Beverly Hills, California. Every day I had to choose how to use those twenty four hours. I could play games like baseball or basketball (no electronic games in those days), listen to the radio, just sit around, or I could choose to invest those hours to better my mind or my relationship with God and others.

Every day of every year throughout the world, each person chooses how to use this gift of time. What makes people different is not the amount of time received each day but how that time is used.

The mission of stewardship is to use our allocation of time, together with our God given talents and resources, to best serve our Creator. We are all called to be grateful and generous stewards of God's gifts.

Grateful Stewards

The year was 1999, just before the dreaded turn of the century which was to wipe out all of humanity, or at least create enormous damage. My wife, Suzanne and I were living in Yorba Linda, California, the place that houses President Nixon's Presidential Library.

Our children were grown and gone from our house, but Suzanne's eighty-six year old dad, Jim, was living with us. Jim was legally blind due to macular degeneration, so we were looking after him after Suzanne's mom had recently passed away.

Before moving to Yorba Linda we had attended, for seventeen years, the large church lead by Pastor Chuck Swindoll. He had left that Church in Fullerton just before we left and moved to Yorba Linda.

Desiring a new church, we were now attending a small church in Yorba Linda, let's give it the name "Deceitful Church" to protect the guilty. Deceitful Church was pastored by a young man named Paul (fictitious of course), who had taken over the pastorate from his dad, Peter. Peter had founded the Church many years earlier and was still very active in the Church. Peter and I became good friends.

I was jogging for long distances in those days because I had time on my hands, since I had completed the management of my last troubled financial institution. After it was sold, there were no more banks to manage on my horizon. The banking crisis had essentially ended in the United States.

It seemed that each day as I was jogging, I would pass Peter who was walking. He lived near me. We would stop and talk but would invariably end up in prayer together on the streets of Yorba Linda. I admired Peter a lot.

I was not earning a paycheck in those days and my wife Suzanne was an elementary school teacher in Yorba Linda. We lived mainly off our savings, as elementary school teachers are not well paid.

An old business acquaintance and banking customer, George (his real name), called and asked for my help in arranging what had proved to be a difficult to obtain bank loan. I still had my banking contacts and still maintained some influence and expertise, so I put together an introduction to the President of the chosen bank, made the proper presentation and recommendation. George soon had his loan.

Afterwards, over lunch in Beverly Hills, George presented me with an unexpected check in the amount of forty thousand dollars for my help. He insisted that I take it. I didn't need a lot of persuasion. He was wealthy and the loan had been large, complicated and difficult for most people to obtain.

Also, Suzanne and I could use the money.

As we prayed about what to do with this financial windfall, my wife and I became convinced that we should donate it all to God through the little Deceitful Church we were then attending. It would be a sacrificial gift since I wasn't earning a paycheck, and there were no prospects for me to do so.

The following Sunday we dropped a check for forty thousand dollars into the offering plate as it was passed.

That same Sunday afternoon I received a call from Pastor Paul, who thanked us for the gift and asked how we wanted the money spent. I simply said that Suzanne and I had given the gift to God through Deceitful Church and that the Church should decide how best to spend the money.

We soon moved on to La Mesa, California and I joined the staff of Shadow Mountain Community Church as the Chief Financial Officer and Chief Operations Officer. David Jeremiah is the Senior Pastor of Shadow Mountain Church.

Peter and I maintained contact, and occasionally Suzanne and I would visit the small Church in Yorba Linda, which was about a two-hour drive from our La Mesa home.

Invariably we would pray with Peter and his wife as we went to dinner with them or visited with them in their home, which was surprisingly expensive for a Pastor.

A few years later I received a call from Peter, who said that he and his family were having difficulty and asked if I could help. He sounded desperate so I responded with a visit to Yorba Linda. As it turned out Peter, Paul and Mary (Paul's wife) had been accused of stealing money from Deceitful Church, almost from its inception. Mary acted as the Church Treasurer.

After a short investigation and, as you can imagine, a lot of very negative publicity, the two pastors pleaded guilty, were convicted and went to prison. The amount misappropriated exceeded three million dollars according to the news reports. I now understood about the expensive home.

Was our forty thousand dollar gift among the monies misused by the two Pastors? In all probability it was, but I never bothered to ask or investigate that question. If it was, does this mean that we should not have donated the money?

Absolutely not! To this day we are grateful that we gave that gift. Our gift was to God, not to the church and certainly not to Peter, Paul and Mary. That gift may well have helped lead to their eventual exposure.

Followers of Jesus Christ should seek to be grateful people who recognize that everything we have has been given to us by God. As grateful beneficiaries, we should strive to honor God by being faithful stewards of all the time, talent, and treasure He has entrusted to us.

We are responsible to God, the local church and to those He has called us to reach in our community and around the world. We realize that God cares about our finances because he cares about our hearts and, therefore, we should embrace all financial issues as spiritual issues.

God uses us, although He does not need us, to share in His Kingdom work so that we may share His joy which comes with this work. When we read, study, or teach scripture, this scripture develops biblical stewardship in our lives. Acknowledging that all of scripture is fully God's Word and that it is the ultimate authority for our lives, will accomplish God's will in us and through us, and we will develop into devoted stewards, which is our mission.

"It is the same with my word. I send it out, and it always produces fruit. It will accomplish all I want it to, and it will prosper everywhere I send it." Isaiah 55:11

Generous Stewards

Years ago, a preacher had been asked to speak at a small church in Tallahassee. As the story was told to me, the preacher, Pastor Ken, had forgotten to pack his tooth brush so he went to the local Publix's grocery store to purchase one on Saturday evening before speaking on Sunday.

While standing in line he noticed the family standing in front of him. The three looked shabby, tired and distraught. They had very few items but it appeared they did not have enough money to pay for their items. Pastor Ken told the clerk that he was paying for the man's groceries. The man turned and looked at the Pastor in bewilderment, but accepted the generous offer.

Two years later, Pastor Ken had been again invited to speak at the small North Florida Church. Following the service, a man and his family walked up to Ken and the man related this story:

"Several years ago, my wife and our child were at the end of our rope, totally destitute. We had lost almost everything; we had no jobs, no money and we were living in our car.

"We had given up all hope, and therefore we had agreed to a plan to end our lives. This plan included our young son who could not have survived without us. However, we decided to first buy our son some food with the little money we had left, since he had not eaten in days. Kind of a last meal. We drove to a nearby grocery store using some of what was left of our gas."

"While we were waiting to pay for our items at the grocery store, we discovered that we did not even have enough money to pay for the food. A man, who was also waiting in line, asked us to please let him pay for our food. This man told us that he was doing it in the name of Jesus."

"We left the store and drove to our prearranged suicide site. We wept. We kept thinking about the act of kindness shown to us at the grocery and about the statement "In the name of Jesus", so we couldn't go through with our suicide plan. We thought that there may be hope after all, so we drove away and parked for the night in the closest parking lot we could locate."

"We awoke the next morning to the sounds of cars coming into the small parking lot. As we looked out we discovered that it was parking for a small church. A sign in front of the church read: Jesus Loves You."

"We went to that little church since it was Sunday, and both my wife and I were saved. Our lives have improved immeasurably since that day. I have a job, we have a place to live, and we can pay for our food. God has greatly blessed us."

He then told the pastor, "When you began to speak this morning, I thought that you were possibly the man who gave us that money at the grocery.

Then as I looked closer I knew for sure that you were that man. The Aussie accent clinched it."

The man continued, "Because of your act of kindness three people are alive physically, and will be with God eternally".[i]

Tears of joy fell from Ken's eyes.

God is a loving God who revealed His limitless generosity through His gift of Jesus Christ. Therefore, we desire to glorify Him by being a generous people.

Seek to operate with an attitude of abundance, believing we have everything we need in time, talent, and treasure for every good work. Also seek to develop generous hearts and teach principles of responsible stewardship through every act of generosity and every ministry of the church.

We should be obedient to God by faithfully giving to support His work in our church and ministries. We should also look for ways to demonstrate the love of Jesus Christ, glorify God and meet the needs of others through acts of generosity in our needy world.

As pastors/teachers of God's Word, our calling is to equip the saints to do the work of ministry (*Ephesians 4*) and correctly explain the word of Truth (*2 Timothy 2:15*). The Apostle Paul, as he writes to the young Pastor Timothy speaks directly to this issue of what to teach a congregation about money. He says:

> *"Teach those who are rich in this world not to be proud and not to trust in their money, which is so unreliable. Their trust should be in God, who richly gives us all we need for our enjoyment.*

Tell them to use their money to do good. They should be rich in good works and generous to those in need, always being ready to share with others. By doing this they will be storing up their treasure as a good foundation for the future so that they may experience true life." I Timothy 6:17-19

Paul gives both warnings and recommendations regarding money. He is careful to warn us about money's powerful ability to confuse our belief systems and tempt us down dangerous paths. Many times, the presence of wealth can change how people view life, view themselves and how they view God.

(See Luke 12:13-31; Luke 16:13)

"But people who long to be rich fall into temptation and are trapped by many foolish and harmful desires that plunge them into ruin and destruction. For the love of money is the root of all kinds of evil. And some people, craving money, have wandered from the true faith and pierced themselves with many sorrows." I Timothy 6:9-10

In I Timothy 6:17-19 Paul also shares how we are to be proactive and generous with our money. Rather than hoarding, squandering or wasting money, Paul admonishes us to use our money to do good, be rich in good works, and always be generous and willing to share. Ultimately, there will be significant blessings we will realize in both this life and the life to come.

The primary motivation we carry into our teaching is the same as Paul's. We are teachers who care for our flock and we teach about biblical giving because we want good things *for* our people not *from* them.

Paul said to the Philippians regarding their giving to God's work:

"I don't say this because I want a gift from you. Rather, I want you to receive a reward for your kindness." Philippians 4:17

As much as we live in the reality that resources are a vital component to ministry, the first priority in giving is always the heart of the giver.

"Whatever you give is acceptable if you give it eagerly." 2 Corinthians 8:12

You have not lived until you have done something for someone who can never repay you. — John Bunyan

GENESIS

In the Introduction chapter, I wrote that this book was written on my heart over a period of four decades. In reality, the genesis of this book comes from the story of my life experiences, which span over seven decades. You see, it took God most of my lifetime to teach me about stewardship. Please allow me to share part of that journey with you, and four big lessons that God taught me regarding stewardship.

The year was 1963. John F. Kennedy was President of the United States and our country had a military draft. Once a boy turned eighteen years of age and became a man under the law, he had to register for the draft. Once registered, he would be assigned a priority number decided by random selection. The lower the number, the sooner you would be drafted into the army. I registered and my draft number was about as low as it could be. The number twenty-four.

However, if you went to college you could get a deferment from the draft. With things beginning to heat up in Viet Nam and elsewhere, college was absolutely the way to go. I had just graduated from Columbus High School in Columbus, Georgia. Columbus' only claims to fame was its army base, Fort Benning, the Chattahoochee River, and the infamous Phoenix City, Alabama across the river. Not much to brag about, but having lived near this army base for the first eighteen years of my life, I was certain that I did not want to be in the US Army.

There was no college in Columbus, Georgia at that time. Most of my classmates went off to colleges in Atlanta or other large cities. I simply could not afford to do that. However, my dad had lost his job as a pressman for the local newspaper, the Columbus Ledger Enquirer, and had taken a job in Memphis. He said that I could move to Memphis, just stay in Columbus, or do whatever I wanted. We were not close to say the least. He was an abusive, foul mouth person, and a heavy drinker.

It was clear to me that I was now on my own. But, there was a college in Memphis … Memphis State University. Since I was paying for college, the idea of a rent-free place to live with a State College nearby had great appeal. I reasoned that I could live with my parents for at least the time it took to go to college, and avoid the draft. I moved to Memphis, Tennessee during the summer of 1963.

Shortly after arriving in Memphis, I was dating the girl next door … Kay. We had been out on the town, most probably to Corky's BBQ or Krystal Burgers, and were driving home in my older brother Bill's 1957 Mercury. Bill had joined the Navy two years earlier and was not living at home. My younger sister and Kay's brother were in the back seat of the Mercury.

The rain was such that you could barely see beyond the front of your car. If you have ever lived in the South during the summer you know about this situation. Had I been wise I would have pulled over and waited for the rain to let up. But, hey, I was eighteen years old and invincible. While passing over a bridge, just before driving past the home of Elvis Presley, I saw it.

Another car was dead stopped on the bridge with no lights on. By the time I saw it, it was clear to me that I could not stop in time to avoid a rear-end collision. I had a split second to make a decision. Hit the car or take evasive action.

There were two lanes of traffic in each direction. We were in the middle lane. I quickly glanced to my right only to see an eighteen wheeler coming up to pass on my right. Swerving right was not an option. Looking into the lane of oncoming traffic it appeared that the lane next to me on my left was clear.

I swerved to the left. As soon as I did, it was too late to change direction. The oncoming car that had been blocked from my vision by the stopped vehicle and the rain was in my face.

We collided.

The two occupants of the small car that I had hit flew out of the front windshield of their car and onto the pavement. I was thrown into the steering wheel; it broke and went through my arm rather than through my chest. Thankfully Kay only received a bump and a cut on her chin, and my sister and Kay's brother were shaken-up but unharmed.

My brother's Mercury was by far the larger car and sustained less damage, but it was totaled. I, and the two men from the other car, ended up in the hospital. I was only there for a few days but the men from the other car were hospitalized for a longer time.

The event made the front page of the Memphis newspaper the next morning, complete with a large photo of me and the crash. The occupants of the oncoming car had been the Mayor of Memphis and the President of Memphis State University. (You can't make this stuff up.) The Mayor had been adamantly opposed to mandatory seatbelt laws. The crash had changed his position on the issue. It was news in Memphis.

With no car to drive, no job, and believing that Memphis State University was not an option after putting its President through a windshield, I was feeling desperate. Besides, in all the chaos, I had missed the deadline to register for college. I was going to be drafted in a matter of weeks, if not days.

After much fervent prayer, I joined the US Navy. This was a turning point in my young life, and my first major lesson in stewardship.

God arranges the circumstances of our life. We are to follow obediently as He leads.

The Navy recruiter gave me a choice for boot camp – the Great Lakes or San Diego, California. Since it was late October and winter was setting in, of course I chose San Diego. The US Navy gave me a plane ticket to California. I had never been on a plane.

I left Memphis with $2.32 in my pocket and the clothes on my back, but convinced that this was God's will for my life. Arriving at boot camp in San Diego, I had to ship my clothes home, and the Navy issued me uniforms. Except, I had to pay for the uniforms. Who knew?

Since I was earning exactly $83.20 per month, it took most all of my pay during boot camp to pay for those uniforms. Because the Navy provided food and shelter, and I could not leave the base, I did not need money. But yes, it bothered me that the Navy made me wear their uniforms, and then required that I work four months to pay for my uniforms. I began to wonder if God was really in this decision to join the Navy.

That question was answered for me a year later, while I was stationed aboard a ship in San Diego. I met my future wife, Suzanne McQuade. A beautiful young and vibrant San Diego State College student. Suzanne and I dated, and then married eighteen months later on July 9, 1966. A major turning point in my life and an answer to my prayers.

I served mostly in Viet Nam during my service, and finished my naval career in Special Forces, stationed at the Navy amphibious base in Coronado, California.

Because the US Navy had invested so much in my training, and because my skills were in demand in Viet Nam, they offered me a twenty thousand dollar tax-free bonus to serve for four more years in Special Forces.

One could actually purchase a fairly decent house for twenty thousand dollars in 1967. But, I was ready for college and the opportunity to do more than serve in combat. Besides, I was convinced that I would never survive another four years in Viet Nam. It was the end of October 1967 when the Navy discharged me. Suzanne had recently given birth to our first child, Jenny Elizabeth.

Once released from the Navy, where I was then earning $211.50 per month, I found a job in electronics earning $311.40 per month, almost a 50% pay increase. Our house rent was only $90 per month, so we were making it, but just barely. Any unexpected expense would be a financial disaster. I can still remember searching under the sofa cushions and in the car for enough change to allow us to go see a movie. At that time we had no TV because we could not afford to buy a TV, or anything else of significance. However, we were extremely happy and somehow we never thought of ourselves as poor. We were poor, but we were content. This led to my second lesson in stewardship:

Be content with what God has provided.

San Diego was home to San Diego State College (now University) where Suzanne had been a student. I applied for admission. They rejected me. Viet Nam veterans were not popular with colleges during 1968, especially Special Forces veterans. I signed up for junior college. They accepted me. They take anybody. And that is a very good thing.

I began classes, but my first college class instructor informed me right away that I was just not college material, and that I should rethink the whole college thing. I couldn't disagree, so I quit. After working all day it was difficult to attend classes all evening.

There is a purpose to this story that has to do with stewardship, and the writing of this book, so please keep reading. We're getting there. Currently I am describing that rags to riches (from a middle class prospective) portion of my life when I received my third big lesson in stewardship.

No one in my family had ever gone to college. My dad had an education only through the third grade. He could barely read. But I had this unexplainable drive to get a college education, however I had exhausted my ability to do so. I mean, three strikes and you are out. That is generally how things work.

At this point I prayed and turned the whole college education possibility over to God. I prayed that if He wanted me to get a college education He would have to make it happen. I had exhausted my attempts.

Another turning point in my life.

Now working the night shift to earn a little extra money, I found that many of my co-workers were going to college during the day. I was encouraged by them to give college another try. I registered for day classes at the same Grossmont Junior College that I had earlier quit.

But this time something was drastically different!

Somehow I had developed a photographic memory. I had never possessed a photographic memory and I don't have one today. But without a doubt I had one then.

Soon I was taking a double load of classes, up to 21 units a semester. I was working over 60 hours per week doing electronics at a Navy facility on North Island, California. I had a family to support, and with the birth of our son, James Louis, we were now a family of four.

My extraordinary wife had to actually drive herself to the hospital to give birth to Jim. I was at work on North Island and the only way home in those days, was via ferry boat which only ran every two hours at night. I made it to the hospital in time for Jim's birth, and thankfully I was able to later drive them both home from the hospital, so that Suzanne did not have to do that on her own.

My routine Monday through Friday was to begin college classes starting at 8 AM, attend class until early afternoon, then take the ferry boat to North Island to clock in at 4 PM for work. Returning home at around 4 AM, I would study using my newfound memory, grab some sleep in the "lazy boy" recliner, then begin over again at 8 AM.

I would take care of things around the house on Saturday, go to Church on Sunday to teach a Sunday school class, and worship both Sunday morning and Sunday night. Over these years, I was a deacon, a trustee and the church treasurer.

All of this I could handle and still receive top grades at college because of the newly acquired gift of memory. After achieving a perfect grade point average at junior college for one year, I again applied to San Diego State. They actually accepted me on this attempt.

Two years later, I graduated *Summa Cum Laude* and at the top of my graduating class of 5000 students. Truly and undoubtedly a gift from God. I called it a miracle. God gets all of the praise for this happening in my life.

The President of San Diego State University, the very college that had rejected me three years earlier, asked me to speak at graduation ceremonies. I was unable to attend my graduation as I had begun a new job by that time.

As I was about to complete college I sought council from my Pastor at the Lemon Grove First Baptist Church my family and I were attending. I told Pastor Bob Kleinschmidt that God had given me the gift of a college education, and asked if he knew how one uses a degree in accounting in God's ministry.

He told me that the Southern Baptist Foreign Mission Board (now the International Mission Board) occasionally used businessmen to administer the business affairs of their mission offices in major mission fields.

With the encouragement of Pastor Kleinschmidt, my wife and I drove an old retired Greyhound diesel bus, loaded with young people from the Lemon Grove church, to Foreign Missions Week at a Glorietta, New Mexico Southern Baptist Conference Center. While there Suzanne and I interviewed many missionaries, listened to testimonies from missionaries, and spoke privately over lunch with the leader of the Mission Board, Dr. Baker James Cauthen and his wife, Eloise. After much fervent prayer, we volunteered to become Southern Baptist missionaries.

Another turning point in my life. Isn't it amazing that my turning points all occurred following fervent prayer?

Suzanne and I knew in our hearts that God was definitely in this decision. However, the Southern Baptist Foreign Mission Board (FMB) representative told me that since all of my work experience had been in electronics, I had to have at least two years' work experience in business before they would take us. This was because I would be working in business administration with the FMB.

Stanford University offered me a full scholarship due to my academic achievements, but that would not have provided the work experience that was required by the FMB.

Rejecting the Stanford opportunity, I immediately went to work with one of the premier public accounting firms in the world, and became a Certified Public Accountant. My thinking was to obtain the two years of business work experience required by the FMB, and become a CPA at the same time.

However, following my certification, a client of the firm offered me a great job with great pay. The company was a real estate and financial pillar of the San Diego community.

After accepting the job, I quickly became one of the highest paid financial executives in a publicly traded company in San Diego, California, earning $50,000 per year plus benefits, such as a company car, corner office and a liberal expense account. I was having fun and making pretty good money for a kid not yet thirty who had grown up poor in Georgia.

Certainly a great improvement over the Navy starting pay ten years earlier of $83.20 per month, and my first civilian job pay of $311.40 per month. It even beat the twenty thousand dollar bonus offered by the US Navy. No more searching the sofa cushions for change, and we could not only afford a nice TV, but also we purchased a beautiful new four bedroom home. That photographic memory thing was still working well.

Every year the representative from the FMB would visit us in our San Diego home and inquire as to our readiness to begin our missionary work. We kept saying, "Maybe next year."

Finally, the mission board told us that if we were to ever become missionaries with the Southern Baptists we had to do it right away, given the age of our children. The FMB did not allow families to go to the mission field for the first time with teenage children. The adjustment was too difficult. Jenny, our daughter, was 11 but would be almost 13 when we got to Peru, if we began right away. Our son Jim was seven.

I now had almost seven years of business work experience, so I was qualified for business administration work according to the FMB guidelines. We prayed as a family for two weeks as we vacationed across America in a motor home.

We came to a decision as a family to become missionaries. I had been studying stewardship in the Bible and was impressed that God wanted my whole heart. Unlike the rich young ruler, written about in the Bible, I was determined to choose Jesus, even if that meant abandoning everything. Suzanne was with me all the way. Our two children were understandably hesitant and a little fearful, but they were on-board.

Leaving the high paying job, we sold the house, cars and just about everything we owned, and set out for Seminary in Fort Worth, Texas during June of 1978. We left San Diego driving a small Ryder rental van loaded with the few belongings we would be shipping to Peru following seminary training.

We kept just enough money to live on until we reached Peru, which was to be about two years later. The FMB would begin paying us $900 per month, but only after we arrived in Peru. Suzanne and I were required to first attend seminary training at a Southern Baptist seminary, and then attend language study for a year in Costa Rica. This was our riches to rags episode.

We were ridiculed enormously by family and even many friends, but that act of surrendering everything to God was a liberating experience.

To abandon money, possessions, a promising career, family and friends, to follow Yeshua was the correct decision in our hearts and minds. We were all in, and it felt good. We actually felt better about this riches to rags episode than we did about the rags to riches event in our lives. We were confident that the decision was right for us.

Our hearts had been captured by God's amazing grace, and we acknowledged that all we had was really His. This was my third big lesson in becoming God's steward.

God owns it all. We are His stewards. We must be willing to give whatever He directs. With joy.

"Then Peter began to say to Him. "See, we have left all and followed You." So Jesus answered and said, "Assuredly, I say to you, there is no one who has left house or brothers or sisters or father or mother or wife or children or lands, for My sake and the gospel's, who shall not receive a hundredfold now in this time – houses and brothers and sisters and mothers and children and lands, with persecutions – and in the age to come, eternal life." Mark 10:28 – 30

My life is a personal testimony to the truth of Jesus' words.

As events evolved into a spiritually rich journey filled with learning about being God's steward, I took notes concerning what God was teaching me about stewardship. Those hand-written notes, from studying and experiencing stewardship during this time, later formed the basis for my teaching stewardship at a Christian University, for writing the stewardship white paper at Mariners Church, and for writing this book.

Due to circumstances, our family left Peru, and returned to California during December 1980.

The journey continued....

Leap forward to the autumn of 1997, when I went with several of my California Baptist University business students to the Federal Court in Riverside, California to attend the sentencing hearing of Harry Houdini (obviously a fictitious name, but the facts are true), a former business associate.

I wanted my students to experience firsthand that there are times when even "white collar crime" gets punished in the United States. After seven years of fighting the legal system through his high-priced attorneys, Houdini had just pled guilty to six counts of misappropriation of funds in a federal criminal case.

This was the last in a series of such cases in which I had made the criminal referrals to the F.B.I. I was a federal witness in this case and the person most responsible for exposing Houdini's crimes.

Originally I never intend to get involved in activities that would lead to criminal prosecution, things just happened. You see, as a businessman, really an accountant, who, through no design of my own, got into the business of turnaround management of savings and loans, I was thrown into a sea of corruption.

It happened to be during the period described by L. William Seidman, former head of the FDIC in the Reagan and Bush administrations, as "the great S&L debacle". Some writers have described the savings and loan (S&L) industry in the 1980s and 1990's as the "worst public scandal in American history".

I was in the middle of this mess.

Mike (again a fictitious name), a self-proclaimed Christian, had built a substantial real estate company, owning and managing over a billion dollars of apartments nationwide.

At the end of 1984 Mike told me he had been trying unsuccessfully for almost two years to acquire an S&L. Since I had negotiated the acquisition of several Savings & Loans for some of my financial and real estate clients, he asked: "Would I help?"

By May 1985 Mike and his two partners were the proud owners of a Savings & Loan. This S&L was an operational disaster and generating significant losses each month, but the price was right, and its deposits were government (FSLIC) insured. By this time the only S&L's available for purchase were at the bottom of the barrel in an industry that was on its death bed.

Mike asked me to become the S&L's CEO and President, fix its problems, and make it profitable. As one who finds it difficult to avoid challenging situations I accepted his offer.

As part of the acquisition of the S&L, the government regulators had agreed that Mike and his partners could use twenty-five million of the S&L's deposits to set up a real estate company that they would run separate from the S&L operation.

The regulators apparently liked what Mike and his partners had done with their other real estate company, and I'm sure the regulators hoped Mike would produce great profits for the S&L, as well as for himself, through this FSLIC insured deposit funded company. The twenty-five million dollars was a large portion of the S&L's assets.

Determined to make Mike's S&L the best, most profitable S&L in California, I threw myself into this project. The twenty-five million was funded immediately to set up the subsidiary company managed by Mike and his partners. Within months my new management team and I had solved many of the savings and loan's operational problems and were making a profit ... or so we thought.

We couldn't seem to get documentation from Mike and his partners regarding their use of the twenty-five million dollars. Such information was required by the S&L regulators.

After much digging, I soon discovered that they had purchased apartments in Georgia, Texas and other states on a highly leveraged basis at prices that appeared to be above market value. At this point the details get complicated. They aren't important. The bottom line is that, using my photographic memory to examine hundreds if not thousands of documents, I soon pieced together what had happened and it wasn't good.

I confronted those I thought responsible, and I notified the regulators of the issues I had uncovered. Mike and his partners lost their ownership of the S&L. Their other company collapsed. The S&L was eventually merged into another financial institution.

Newspaper headlines called this: "The biggest real-estate syndication failure in California history". The FBI commenced an investigation.

After this, and over the ensuing years, I gained a reputation with bank regulators as somewhat bright, extremely honest, and as a stand-up kind of businessman who wouldn't run from problems.

With the S&L industry now in turmoil and the regulatory ranks thin, the regulators were pleased to recommend me to become involved with other problem Saving and Loan situations. Thus began a fifteen year career of repairing dysfunctional financial institutions, exposing wrong when I found it, and working with our criminal justice system to help prosecute criminals. One of these situations resulted in a federal criminal case involving Houdini.

At the beginning of this saga, Houdini called me at home. He had been given my number by a high ranking federal bank examiner.

The savings and loan he owned was having management problems according to the Federal and California State regulators. Houdini needed help to solve the problems and therefore keep the regulators satisfied with the operation and performance of his S&L.

Having just completed the workout of a Beverly Hills based savings and loan, I was ready for the next challenge. Arriving at the S&L's executive offices on the fifth floor of a mid-rise office building bearing the S&L's name, I was intrigued. Since the executive offices occupied the entire fifth floor, I entered the reception area as I exited the elevator. The walls were lined with posters.

Investigating the posters, I thought at first they were of circus acts. I looked closer. No, they were framed playbills, prints and posters of magicians. I thought this strange decor for a financial institution. It wasn't the last thing I found strange about this financial institution or its owner.

Houdini and I had lunch. We seemed to hit it off. I liked him and I found him intelligent, friendly and quite enjoyable to talk with; although he did go a bit overboard trying to impress me with who he knew and what he had accomplished. Among the things of significance, he counted among his personal friends U.S. Senators Alan Cranston and Ted Kennedy. I don't know if this was true or not. I never met the Senators.

Days later Houdini asked to have lunch again. He had a proposal. On October 20, 1989, I entered the savings and loan's fifth floor reception area as its new President and CEO.

If one were to ask Houdini today, what life decisions he would like most to reverse, I'm sure that his decision to hire George Hale as President of his S&L would rank near the top. Probably at the top.

Before he hired me however, I gave Houdini, and the other Directors of the S&L, what by then had become my standard warning: "If you've done anything wrong at your S&L, or if you plan to do anything wrong, I'm the last person you want to put in charge. I have zero tolerance for criminal, immoral or unethical behavior. If it exists, I will invariably uncover and expose it".

I've often thought that I must look stupid. It seems that no one ever heeds my warning. Houdini was no exception. The Directors recorded my warning into the minute book and promptly hired me as CEO, at Houdini's insistence.

Two months later (yes, only two months later) I handed the Los Angeles office of the FBI a criminal referral documenting Houdini's systematic looting of his savings & loan, and ultimately the American taxpayer, out of approximately $200 million, over the prior six years.

This fraud had eluded discovery by every bank examiner, both state and federal, who had annually examined the S & L, and by the auditors from one of the largest and most prestigious accounting firms in the world, who annually had given their opinion as to the fairness of the S & L's financials. Houdini was a magician. However, I still possessed a God given photographic memory, and this triumphed over magic.

As a result of my discoveries, criminal referrals, and the subsequent FBI investigation, three California financial institutions were seized, including Houdini's savings and loan. There was some national publicity about these events. Each of the TV networks reported the story multiple times, and it was featured on shows such as Sixty Minutes and 20/20. *The New York Times*, *The Los Angeles Times,* and *The Wall Street Journal* ran lengthy front page articles.

No one covered one of the underlying tragedies. There were scores of people, most of whom would never consider stealing for themselves, who elected to look the other way, even participate in the crime and/or the subsequent cover-up. Some claimed to be Christians. The wife of one of the co-conspirators actually came by my office during the investigation to tell me that her husband could not possibly be involved in anything criminal. After all she said: "He was a devoted Christian".

I've seen this same behavior in dozens of similar situations. The few who cheat, steal, or don't play by the rules, and the many who seem to accept it, condone it, or even encourage it by their own actions or inactions. Not only are they not ashamed of their, or their colleague's behavior, they ridicule those who see it as wrong and who want to stop it. By their silence they condone the behavior, perhaps even allowing it to continue, and through silence, they also embolden others to do the same thing. Some of these enablers are eager to call themselves Christian.

Someone once said; "The only thing necessary for the triumph of evil is that good men should do nothing." The origin of this quote is disputed; some say it was Edmund Burke, others say the Rev. Charles Aked. Its application is inescapable.

Several years ago, I consulted on some business matters with a Christian businessman who was just starting his own company after over 20 successful years of working for large corporations. As I'm prone to do, I brought the conversation around to God's pattern for Christians in business.

Gary said, "I'm not going to let it be known that I'm a Christian businessman, or that I operate a Christian business." Gary's wife, a non-Christian, had some unpleasant experiences with businesses proclaiming themselves "Christian". Now, when she encounters the "fish sign", she runs the other way.

Apparently she believes that most businesspeople who advertise their Christianity do so to suck the customer into using their business and trusting them beyond the bounds the customer would trust a non-Christian business. The "Christian" business then takes advantage of the over trusting customer. Sad, isn't it? But all too often true.

Ben is a prime example. (Another fictitious name). When I first met Ben in 1977, just before I left California for work as a missionary, he was leading a sizable weekly Bible study and prayer breakfast for Christians in business. He also owned and managed his own home improvement and construction business.

Most words out of Ben's mouth were his quoting of scripture. He always had a smile, a handshake, and an encouraging word. He was always willing to pray with and for you. Ben had an infectious, upbeat, positive attitude at all times. The picture of a victorious Christian.

The last time I saw Ben was 1993 in a California courtroom. Ben had just lost a multi-million dollar lawsuit he had filed against one of my ex-clients, whom I had introduced to Ben. I was a witness in the trial.

This had been the second trial for the same lawsuit. In the first trial Ben had won a large dollar judgement - millions. Fortunately for Bob, my ex-client, the judge vacated his judgement and recused himself from the case two days after his judgement. As was later disclosed, this Christian judge had apparently received a "pay-off" from Ben's Christian attorney.

Non-Christian Bob was now no longer puzzled as to why Ben and his attorney had waived their right to a jury trial. Needless to say, Bob's attorney insisted on having a jury for the second trial.

The FBI announced their investigation into the judge's activities the day after his announced judgement in Ben's case against Bob. As reported in the news, the judge had been accused of a pattern of receiving such "pay-offs" from Ben's attorney and others.

The newspaper also later reported that this judge shot and killed himself while in a cheap motel room in another city, the day before his indictment was to be announced. Ben's attorney was also discovered dead in his swimming pool just a short time after he lost the second trial. He had drowned, although he was an excellent swimmer by all accounts. Just a coincidence? Perhaps so, but two more persons touched by Ben's life and business activities. The list is long.

Bob actually considers himself fortunate that all he lost was the four million dollars he had invested with Ben and the two million dollars in legal fees for defending the lawsuit, including the two trials that stretched over eight years. He could afford such a monetary loss.

The jury found that Ben's lawsuit was malicious and rewarded Bob with a two million dollar judgement for his legal fees. Bob never tried to collect on this judgement as Ben left the State.

Is there an answer to this activity of claiming to be a Christ follower, but living a far different life-style? A life demonstrated by the immoral, unethical and illegal business behavior which I have just described in the episodes written about above?

First, let me assure you that God will deal with the Mike's, Ben's, Houdini's, and the many who stand by and do nothing as evil happens, just as He will deal with each of us.

We are all accountable:

"But you, why do you judge your brother? Or you again, why do you regard your brother with contempt? For we shall all stand before the judgement seat of God. For it is written, "As I live, says the Lord, every knee shall bow to Me, and every tongue shall give praise to God." So then each one of us shall give account of himself to God." Romans 14:10-12.

Second, let me say that our concern is not with the non-Christian business person, like Houdini, nor is it with the business person who calls himself Christian and acts like it doesn't matter, such as Ben. Our concern is with ourselves. How do I live, how do I conduct business or perform my job, and how do I manage God's assets.

If you share my concern, then I'm telling you that yes, God really does have a solution. A plan, that if followed will not only result in moral and ethical behavior, but will produce purpose, peace, power and prosperity in the life of the Christian who follows it consistently.

I first began to seriously research this question during 1995 after Dr. Robert Jabs, Chair of the Business Department at California Baptist University (CBU) located in Riverside, California, asked me to teach a class on the subject: "Biblical Principles of Business".

Because of the recommendation of Dr. Jabs, I had just been named to the chair of business ethics at California Baptist University, the Anderson Chair, and I served on the University President's advisory council.

Dr. Jabs and I had become acquaintances during the S&L crisis. He was a Director, on the Board of a sizable Southern California savings and loan. Our paths had crossed, and he was aware of some of my activities of exposing criminals and righting wrongs.

By that time many people working in the financial institutions industry either knew me personally or by reputation. Articles would occasionally appear in newspapers concerning my adventures, and I was a speaker at financial conferences. By 1995 I had been the CEO of ten troubled savings and loans.

Accepting Dr. Jab's offer to teach the class, I reviewed the information that others before me had used while teaching this course. I found that most of the material followed basically the same pattern. Quote a verse of scripture, call it a principle and apply it to work or business. Several of the lists of verses and principles were voluminous. Many verses showed up on all lists.

At times the terms "Biblical principles" and "business ethics" were used interchangeably. Some professors had even invited to their classrooms, Christian businesspeople who spoke about their Biblical principles of business and gave inspiring personal testimonies. The students seemed to have really appreciated meeting and listening to these business leaders. Personal testimonies are always more interesting than lectures. I noted that I would use such testimonies during my classes.

However, after reviewing all of the material I was still a little confused about exactly what God's principles of work and business really were. A few things became crystal clear.

The first was that God, in His Word, devoted much space to the subject of work, money, possessions, stewardship and related topics. I read and was told that in the Bible, there are approximately five hundred verses on prayer, another approximately five hundred verses on faith, and more than two thousand verses dealing with money and possessions.

I didn't try to verify this, but I do know that many of Jesus' parables concerned the subjects of money or possessions.

Therefore I concluded that God must give some importance to these subjects.

Secondly, it finally it hit me that it wasn't solely about Biblical principles of work, but about Biblical principles of stewardship, including work. A subject that I had previously learned much about. The living out of God's principles of stewardship in our daily life.

This realization led to the forth big lesson that God taught me regarding stewardship:

Stewardship is about every aspect of a Christian's life.

It encompasses all that I do after I first accept Jesus Christ as my Lord and Savior. Therefore, after much prayer and study, the following statement captures what I taught to that Biblical Principles of Business class, and to other such classes over the ensuing years:

WE ARE EACH CREATED TO BE GOD'S STEWARD.

FIRST SOME BASICS:

A **precept** is:

"A commandment or direction meant as a rule of action or conduct. A rule of moral conduct; a maxim of action or conduct." This is according to *Webster's New World Dictionary.*

A **principle** can be thought of as the reason behind a precept. The fundamental truth upon which a precept is based. Again, according to *Webster's*:

"The ultimate source, origin, or cause of something. A fundamental truth, law, doctrine or motivation force, upon which others are based." Principles therefore are truths that recur throughout scripture that present a larger picture and understanding, and there is a body of teaching on the subject. God has some fundamental truths that He wants us to know and to follow. These truths, or **principles**, relate to every important aspect of our life and reflect God's character and our purpose in life.

God gave His followers certain "rules of conduct" that He expects to be obeyed. These rules, or **precepts** fall into two general categories. The first category consists of commands God gave to a specific people, in a specific situation and for a specific time.

Examples of these temporal precepts are God telling Noah to build an ark (Genesis 6:14), His command to Abraham for the covenant of circumcision (Genesis 17: 9-11), and His command to the Jews to tithe (Numbers 18).

The second category is precepts which are in accordance with God's character or nature – His principles. These are commands for all people, in all situations, and for all times. These are the precepts that concern us.

We are responsible for knowing these rules and complying with them. These precepts serve not only as "a rule of moral conduct" for our lives, but also to point us, and those with whom we have contact, to God's principles and ultimately to God.

God doesn't do anything accidentally, haphazardly, or without purpose. Everything He does, says or creates is perfect and orderly. It all works in harmony with everything else He has said, done or created. What follows in the next chapter is what I came to believe is God's plan and purpose for every believer.

First, to list the life lessons that I learned on my journey:

- **God arranges the circumstances of our life. We are to follow obediently as He leads.**

- **Be content with what God has provided.**

- **God owns it all. We are His stewards. We must be willing to give whatever He directs. With joy.**

- **Stewardship is about every aspect of a Christian's life.**

So God created man in His own image; in the image of God He created him; male and female He created them. Genesis 1:27

CREATED FOR A PURPOSE

God created all things and is Lord of all that He has made. He created each of us to be a steward for a brief moment of eternity over a portion of His creation for the purpose of our knowing God, glorifying God and making God known.

God gave me a purpose in life of being His steward!

> God created us to *"Be fruitful and multiply, and fill the earth, and subdue it; and rule over the fish of the sea and over the birds of the sky, and over every living thing that moves on the earth."* Then God said, *"Behold, I have given you every plant yielding seed that is on the surface of all the earth, and every tree which has fruit yielding seed; it shall be food for you;"* Genesis 1:28-29

In the beginning, written in the very first chapter of Scripture, God gave mankind a vocation and a purpose. However man broke the relationship with God through sin.

Therefore the first step toward again becoming God's steward is the restoration of the relationship. This is called salvation or being born again. Without the servant/master relationship we are merely users of God's assets and not stewards over God's assets.

Let's consider each aspect of our purpose, as written in my stewardship statement at the beginning of this chapter:

- "brief moment"
- "knowing God"
- "glorifying God"
- "making God known"

BRIEF MOMENT

"As for man, his days are like grass; As a flower of the field, so he flourishes. When the wind has passed over it, it is no more; And its place acknowledges it no longer. Psalms 103:15-16.

Come now, you who say, "Today or tomorrow, we shall go to such and such a city, and spend a year there and engage in business and make a profit." Yet you do not know what your life will be like tomorrow. You are just a vapor that appears for a little while and then vanishes away." James 4:13-14.

"Lord, make me to know my end, and what is the extent of my days, let me know how transient I am." Psalms 39:4

Truly, God has given each of us but a moment in time to serve Him on this earth.

Some, like Amy, the daughter of one of my best friends, who died at age 23 of an accidental drug overdose; or like my brother Bill, who died at age 57 of pancreatic cancer, have had a shorter period of time here on earth than, say me ... who at 75 is still going strong, or my friend from the gym, Jimmy, who at age 87 is going even stronger.

Still, in the expanse of time, what is 75 years, or even 87 years? It is but a moment.

The prayer of Moses, as written in Psalm 90:10 states:

"The days of our lives are seventy years, and if by reason of strength they are eighty years."

And the mystery is that no one knows their allotment of time. We need to use every day as if it were our last day ... you never know ... it may be our last day.

William Shatner (Star Trek's Captain Kirk) recorded a song about dying titled "You'll Have Time":

Live life
Live life like you're gonna die
Because you're gonna
I hate to be the bearer of bad news
But you're gonna die

Maybe not today or even next year
But before you know it you'll be saying
"Is this all there was?
What was all the fuss?
Why did I bother?"

Now, maybe you won't suffer maybe it's quick
But you'll have time to think
Why did I waste it?
Why didn't I taste it?
You'll have time
Because you're gonna die.

Not a Christian song but it has a point. Our time on earth is brief and in the end we're all "gonna" die. Statistics bear this out. And, we will take nothing with us to the grave.

Although it is true that you will take nothing to the grave, you can still exercise Biblical stewardship even after you die.

When I was the person responsible for stewardship at Shadow Mountain Community Church, along with Pastor David Jeremiah, I noticed that many of the members were old. We were conducting frequent funerals and memorial services. Most of our members who died left this life with no estate plan – no will or living trust. That meant that the State of California was deciding what to do with the assets that were left. Not a good situation.

I thought that a better idea was for our members to decide before they died who received their estate.

As I was researching a solution to this dilemma, I located a Christian law firm that specialized in preparing Living Trusts for Christians. I contacted the firm and met a man named Mike.

Mike specialized in presenting the need, workings and benefit of estate planning to a Christian audience. Following Mike's presentation, the law firm would provide an hour of consultation *pro bono* for those who requested it. At the end, the person could do nothing, have the law firm prepare a living trust, or have it prepared elsewhere.

They were informed that their Living Trust could designate a Church, such as Shadow Mountain, or another Christian ministry, as the recipient of a portion or all of their estate.

Mike and I made such a presentation for those who were interested at Shadow Mountain Church. The response was awesome. Hundreds attended and scores actually prepared a Living Trust, with many naming Shadow Mountain or other Christian ministries to receive a portion of their estate.

Those who did so were very appreciative of the knowledge they received, the Living Trust that was produced, and the peace and satisfaction of preparing well for their eventual death, including leaving a portion of their estate to a Christian ministry.

As these people passed into eternity, their families were cared for and large donations came into the Kingdom of God. Mike and I put on many such presentations with the same result.

Mike died of cancer a few years later. He had a Living Trust.

Every family should have a Living Trust, but so few do. Check it out. After all, we're all "gonna" die.

KNOW GOD

Our aim is to know God. Not to know *about* God. Paul wrote:

> *"But whatever things were gain to me, those things I have counted as loss for the sake of Christ. More than that, I count all things to be loss in view of the surpassing value of knowing Christ Jesus my Lord, for whom I have suffered the loss of all things, and count them but rubbish in order that I may gain Christ, and may be found in Him, ... that I may know Him."*
> Philippians 3:7-10

If we seek to know God, we will. Knowing God is a matter of personal involvement with God. **Accept** Jesus Christ as Lord and Savior. **Abide** with Him.

Walk with God daily by reading His word, talking with Him and giving Him praise.

The Problem

As we will explore later in greater detail, three aspects of God's character are His qualities of holiness, mercy and justice.

God is holy and without sin, therefore He cannot fellowship with those who are sinful.

"Thine eyes are too pure to approve evil, and Thou canst not look on wickedness with favor." Habakkuk 1:13

His Word tells us that we are all sinful. *"For all have sinned and fall short of the glory of God."* Romans 3:23.

God is just, therefore He must punish sin. *"For the wages of sin is death ..."* Romans 6:23 a.

God is merciful, and He does not want us to perish. *"The Lord is not slow about His promise, as some count slowness, but is patient toward you, not wishing for any to perish but for all to come to repentance."* II Peter 3:9.

The Solution

God provided a solution to solve this problem for us. He sent Himself, in the form of Jesus Christ, to reconcile us to Himself.

"He made Him who knew no sin to be sin on our behalf that we might become the righteousness of God in Him. Therefor if any man is in Christ, he is a new creature; the old things passed away; behold, new things have come. Now all these things are from God, who reconciled us to Himself through Christ" II Corinthians 5:21 and 17-18

The solution is in place. The reconciliation is complete. Eternal life is ours as a free gift subject only to our acceptance.

"For the wages of sin is death, **but the free gift of God is eternal life in Christ Jesus our Lord."** Romans 6:23 *"For God so loved the world, that He gave His only begotten Son, that whoever believes in Him should not perish, but have eternal life."* John 3:16

But how do we accept this gift?

God tells us that we must confess our sin, repent of our sin, believe in Christ Jesus, and accept Him as our savior and Lord of our life by faith.

"that if you confess with your mouth Jesus {as} Lord, and believe in your heart that God raised Him from the dead, you shall be saved; for with the heart man believes, resulting in righteousness, and with the mouth he confesses, resulting in salvation. For the Scripture says, "Whoever believes in Him will not be disappointed." Rom. 10:9 - 11

"For by grace you have been saved through faith; and not that of yourselves, it is the gift of God" Ephesians 2:8.

Saving faith is trusting in Jesus Christ **alone** for our salvation. This is illustrated in the lives of many, including that of John Wesley. Wesley attended Oxford Seminary for five years, served ten years as a minister of the Church of England, was a missionary to the state of Georgia in 1735, and started the Methodist Church.

Wesley was a man of many good works and very pious. He believed that his works and dedication would gain him heaven. Beginning each day at 4 A.M., with three hours of prayer and Bible study, his day of ministry included trips to the jails and hospitals. He would help others and teach until late each night when he ended his day in prayer. The Methodist Church derives its very name from the pious life that John Wesley lived.

Dr. James Kennedy in the first edition of his book *Evangelism Explosion*, relates this account of John Wesley's salvation:

"On the way back from America there was a great storm at sea. The little ship in which, they were sailing was about to sink. Huge waves broke over the ship deck and the wind shredded the sails. Wesley feared he was going to die that hour and he was terrified. He had no assurance of what would happen to him when he died. Despite all of his efforts to be good, death now for him was a big, black, fearful question mark.

On the other side of the ship was a group of men who were singing hymns. He: asked them, "How can you sing when this very night you are going to die?" They replied, "If this ship goes down we will go up to be with the Lord forever."

Wesley went away shaking his head, thinking to himself, "How can they know that?"

What more have they done than I have done?" Then he added, "I came to convert the heathen, ah, but who shall convert me?"

In the providence of God, the ship made it back to England. Wesley went to London, and found his way to Aldersgate Street and a small chapel. There he heard a man reading a sermon which had been written two centuries earlier by Martin Luther, entitled "Luther's Preface to the Book of Romans."

This sermon described what **real faith** was. It is **trusting Jesus Christ only for salvation-and not in our own good works.**

Wesley suddenly realized that he had been on the wrong road all his life. That night .he wrote these words in his journal: "About a quarter before nine, while he was describing the change which God works in the heart through faith in Christ, I felt my heart strangely warmed. I felt I did trust in Christ, Christ alone, for salvation; and an assurance was given me that He had taken away my sins, even mine, and saved me from the law of sin and death."

There it is. That is saving faith. Repenting of his sins, he trusted in Jesus Christ alone for salvation. Now, would you say that Wesley had not believed in Jesus Christ before this night? Of course, he had.

He was a biblical scholar and had studied about Christ in English, and Latin, and Greek and Hebrew. He had believed in Christ in all these languages. But he trusted in John Wesley for his salvation.

After this he became the greatest preacher of the eighteenth century. But it all began when he put his trust in Jesus Christ alone for his salvation."ⁱⁱ

The first step of knowing God is to accept Him as our Lord and Savior ("justification"). The second step is to abide with Him ("sanctification").

Only the saved or "reborn" person is enabled to see and understand from God's perspective.

> *"But a natural man does not accept the things of the Spirit of God; for they are foolishness to him, and he cannot understand them, because they are spiritually appraised. But he who is spiritual appraises all things, yet he himself is appraised by no man. For who has known the mind of the Lord, that he should instruct Him? But we have the mind of Christ."*
> I Corinthians 2:14 - 16

Our private, daily relationship of worshiping God is the great essential of knowing Him. Our public worth to God is but a reflection of our private relationship with Him. If we do not spend time reading His Word, praising Him, talking with Him, and meditating upon Him, we will not know Him. We will therefore be useless to God, to ourselves, and to others in the everyday stuff of life.

"I am the true vine, and My Father is the vinedresser. Every branch in Me that does not bear fruit, He takes away; and every branch that bears fruit, He prunes it, that it may bear more fruit. You are already clean because of the word which I have spoken to you. Abide in Me, and I in you.

As the branch cannot bear fruit of itself, unless it abides in the vine, so neither can you, unless you abide in Me. I am the vine, you are the branches; he who abides in Me, and I in him, he bears much fruit; for apart from Me you can do nothing.

If anyone does not abide in Me, he is thrown away as a branch, and dries up; and they gather them, and cast them into the fire, and they are burned. If you abide in Me, and My words abide in you, ask whatever you wish, and it shall be done for you." John 15:1-7

THE CONFLICT

From the moment of creation, God knew that there would be conflict and temptation for us to fail to know Him and to thus deviate from His plan. Such temptation and deviation would only increase through the ages as business and possessions multiplied.

In the beginning God gave only one law. Do not eat of the fruit *"...from the tree of the knowledge of good and evil."* Genesis 2:17.

After man violated that command, or precept, God provided an increasingly complex program of revealing Himself. This revealing culminated with Christ's death and resurrection, the giving of the Holy Spirit, and the finished writing of God's Word.

God first taught us like school children learning a new subject. He began with the basics and later introduced the concepts behind these basics.

For example:

In order to learn to communicate through writing, we first learned our ABC's (God's first commands - such as don't eat from the tree of life); we then learned to print the letters (God's Ten Commandments); we put the letters together to form words (The Law given in the Old Testament); and finally, we linked words together to communicate a complete thought or idea (The completed Word of God). Thus the ultimate purpose of learning the ABC's was to teach us to communicate through writing. We had to start with the ABC's.

The ultimate purpose of God was to reveal Himself to man so that we might know Him. He had to start with His commandments or precepts ... The ABC's.

The apostle Paul wrote: *"Why the Law then? It was added because of transgressions, having been ordained through angels by the agency of a mediator, until the seed should come to whom the promise had been made. ...Therefore the Law has become our tutor to lead us to Christ, that we may be justified by faith"*. Galatians 3:19 and 24

The "world", Satan to be more precise, has always warred against God in the life of man for the soul of man. God knew that the winner of this war would, in part, be revealed by man's attitude towards the things of the world.

*"Do not lay up for yourselves treasures upon earth, where moth and rust destroys, and where thieves break in and steal. But lay up for yourselves treasures in heaven, where neither moth nor rust destroys, and where thieves do not break in or steal; **for where your treasure is, there will your heart be also.**"* Matthew 6:19-21

*"No servant can serve two masters; for either he will hate the one, and love the other, or else he will hold to one, and despise the other. **You cannot serve God and mammon**"* Luke 16:13

*"Do not love the world, nor the things in the world. **If anyone loves the world, the love of the Father is not in him**. For all that is in the world, the lust of the flesh and the lust of the eyes and the boastful pride of life, is not from the Father, but is from the world."* I John 2:15-16

Abel brought to God an offering from *"... the firstlings of his flock and of their fat portions. And the Lord had regard for Abel and for his offering."* Genesis 4:4

Cain went through the ritual of an offering to God but I believe he offered God something less than the best, or first of his crops. Cain kept the best for himself. God saw this attitude in Cain and found his offering unacceptable. *"But for Cain and for his offering He had no regard."* Genesis 4:5.

If we are ever to know God, our attitude must be that of Abel.

I am only a sinner that God has saved from the "world" and given an opportunity to know Him. How I use that opportunity depends upon me. However, God did not leave me alone. I am indwelt with the **Holy Spirit** and I have **God's Word**. His Word contains His **Promises.** He will give me **Wisdom** if I ask through **Prayer**.

My responsibility is to abide with Him so that He may teach me and produce Himself in me.

"And by this we know that we have come to know Him, if we keep His commandments. The one who says, "I have come to know Him," and does not keep His commandments, is a liar, and the truth is not in him; but whoever keeps His word, in him the love of God has truly been perfected. By this we know that we are in Him: the one who says he abides in Him ought himself to walk in the same manner as He walked." I John 2:3-6.

Do you want to know God? Do you want peace, purpose, power and prosperity in your life? Accept Jesus Christ alone for your salvation. Abide with God. Know Him. This is His plan. This is your calling as a steward.

GLORIFY GOD

"The faith which saves the soul is not a dead faith, but a faith which operates with purifying effect upon our entire nature, and produces in us fruits of righteousness to the praise and glory of God." Charles H. Spurgeon

"By this is My Father glorified, that you bear much fruit, and so prove to be My disciples." John 15:8

We glorify God and make Him known by "bearing fruit." This "fruit" is God's character.

"But the fruit of the Spirit is love, joy, peace, patience, kindness, goodness, faithfulness, gentleness, self-control; against such there is no law." Galatians 5:22-23

Therefore, the evidence of our love is "fruit" produced by the Holy Spirit

*"You will know them by their fruit. Grapes are not gathered from thorn bushes, nor figs from thistles, are they? Even so, every good tree bears good fruit; but the rotten tree bears bad fruit. A good tree cannot produce bad fruit, nor can a rotten tree produce good fruit. Every tree that does not bear good fruit is cut down and thrown into the fire. So then, **you will know them by their fruit.**"* Matthew 7:16-20

I will explore this fruit-bearing thing a little more in a moment, but for now let's just say that we are to be grape racks.

MAKE GOD KNOWN

"Go therefore and make disciples of all the nations, baptizing them in the name of the Father and the Son and the Holy Spirit, teaching them to observe all that I commanded you; and lo, I am with you always, even to the end of the age." Matthew 28:19 & 20

Making God known is all about evangelism – sharing the gospel with others.

Dr. W. Oscar Thompson was a very special person. I first met Dr. Thompson during 1978 while I was a student at Southwestern Baptist Theological Seminary in Fort Worth, Texas. He was my professor of evangelism.

One day I learned that Dr. Thompson had cancer, he was dying. You could never have discerned this by his countenance. His life was a message of joy. On the Sunday morning after Christmas, 1980, Dr. Thompson was called to be with God.

He taught the message of evangelism through "Concentric Circles". Following his death his wife collected and put into a book some of Dr. Thompson's teaching on this subject, _Concentric Circles of Concern._ I know of no better way to teach how to make God known through our lives, than by sharing some of Dr. Thompson's teaching.

"When the concept of life-style evangelism first began to roll over in my mind, I had been asked to teach an evangelism class for a couple of nights for a friend at a Bible institute. As I drove to class that first night, I kept mulling over this concept in my mind.

I got to the class. As I was thinking through this concept, I drew seven circles on the board. They were like a target with a bull's eye in the center, Concentric Circles. Circle 1 is Self. Circle 2 is Immediate Family. Circle 3 is Relatives. Circle 4 is Close Friends. Circle 5 is Business Associates and Neighbors. Circle 6 is Acquaintances. Circle 7 is Person X.

I said to my class, "The gospel moves on contiguous lines - on lines of relationship." I explained the circles and what each circle represented. "Now," I said, "I believe that God holds you responsible for everyone whom he brings into your sphere of influence. Many of us come to study evangelism to go from Circle 1 out to Circle 7 to salve our consciences because there are ruptured relationships in Circles 2 through 6 that we had rather skip over."

When we have ruptured relationships horizontally, we also have a ruptured relationship vertically, with God. It is not that we do not know the Lord. It is just that he is not really Lord of our lives.

We are not willing to let him be Lord of everything and accept people on his conditions.

With Person X, our life-styles do not have to be consistent. We can talk and then be on our way. There is nothing wrong with telling Person X about Jesus. We are supposed to do that. God will bring these people into our lives; but if we cannot tell people in Circle 2 through 6 about the Lord, we are hypocritical. We are play acting. We are unreal people. If we are genuine, we will want to share with those closest to us."[iii]

God gave us a command in Matthew 28:19 & 20, as quoted above. Just before making this command Jesus wanted to make crystal clear His authority to issue such a command: (v. 18) *"All authority has been given to Me. In heaven and on earth."*

So, God gave each born again believer a command: "make disciples". That means first "share the gospel". He did not say do it if you are comfortable about doing it, if you feel like doing it, or if you are really, really good at doing it. He said "just do it".

Dr. Thompson tells us that effective sharing of the gospel runs along rails of relationships. We are responsible for sharing the gospel with those within our sphere of relationships.

We don't neglect person X as God puts them into our path. Like Pastor Ken in our North Florida story above, it can be through a simple act of kindness in the name of Jesus. As Ken shared "In Jesus' name", three souls were ultimately saved.

This is God's plan ... share the gospel and make disciples.

Are you a participant in God's plan and His purpose for your life?

God discerns the thoughts and intents of our heart and consistently uses three methods to expose if a person is a participant or not in His plan.

"For the word of God is living and active and sharper than any two-edged sword, and piercing as far as the division of soul and spirit, of both joints and marrow, and able to judge the thoughts and intentions of the heart." Hebrews 4:12

1. The first method God uses is to determine a person's attitude toward the things of the world.

2. The second method is to determine if a person follows God's precepts (commandments) and;

3. The third determinate is the "fruit" of a person's life.

Attitude toward the world

Matthew 6:21; 8:21-22; 10:37-39; 16:24-25; 19:16-26; 22:2-8; Mark 8:34-36; 10:17-25; John 15:19; John 17:14-21; Acts 5:1-11; Romans 8:5-8; Romans 12:2; Philippians 3:18-20; I Timothy 6:9-11, 17; James 4:4; I John 2:15

(These are verses for further study.)

Some key verses:

"For where your treasure is, there will your heart be also. Matt 6:21 *And do not be conformed to this world, but be transformed by the renewing of your mind, that you may prove what the will of God is, that which is good and acceptable and perfect."* Romans 12:2

"For many walk, of whom I often told you, and now tell you even weeping, that they are enemies of the cross of Christ, whose end is

destruction, whose god is their appetite, and whose glory is in their shame, who set their minds on earthly things. For our citizenship is in heaven, from which also we eagerly wait for a Savior, the Lord Jesus Christ" Philippians 3:18-20

Have you ever experienced yourself questioning your own motives or attitude about doing a particular thing? Or how about questioning your own motivation for wanting a thing to occur, you know, a certain outcome? I find myself questioning myself like this much of the time. And you know what, sometimes I just can't figure out my own heart motivation. The desired deed or outcome seems righteous, but is my desire similarly righteous? I vacillate back and forth at times trying to answer this question truthfully, since there are often conflicting motivations.

There are times when the service, or the gift I gave, did well but the motivation was, in part, self-serving; my desire to be admired, liked, or recognized. That motivation was pushed down, or even hidden from me, by me. Our hearts are so deceptive. But every gift or deed we give or do, begins in the heart. That is why God addressed the heart so often, and why our attitude is so very important to God.

Our attitude defines who we really are.

Follow God's precepts

Matthew 7:21-23, 24; John 14:15, 21, 23-24; Romans 6:16; Titus 1:16; James 1:22-27; I John 2:3-6; I John 3:10, 24; I John 5:2-3 (Some verses for further study.)

Some key verses:

"Not everyone who says to Me, 'Lord, Lord,' will enter the kingdom of heaven; but he who does the will of My Father who is in heaven.

Many will say to Me on that day, 'Lord, Lord, did we not prophesy in Your name, and in Your name cast out demons, and in Your name perform many miracles? And then I will declare to them, "I never knew you; depart from me you who practice lawlessness." Matthew 7:21-23

"If you love Me, you will keep My commandments." John 14:15

"He who has My commandments and keeps them, he it is who loves Me; and he who loves Me shall be loved by My Father, and I will love him, and will disclose Myself to him." John 14:21

"And by this we know that we have come to know Him, if we keep His commandments. The one who says, "I have come to know Him," and does not keep His commandments, is a liar, and the truth is not in him; but whoever keeps His word, in him the love of God has truly been perfected. By this we know that we are in Him; the one who says he abides in Him ought himself to walk in the same manner as He walked." I John 2:3-6.

Some would say that we are freed from keeping the law or commandments by the sacrifice of Jesus Christ on the cross, and the new covenant. They miss the concept of "keeping the commandments". The term "keeping the commandments" is actually a nautical term.

When I was in the US Navy, my ship assignment was to the USS Seminole AKA 104, an attack cargo ship. The year was early 1965 and we were ordered to land some of the first marines onto the shores of Viet Nam.

We had to cruise from San Diego to Viet Nam, with a stopover in Hawaii to pick up about 1200 marines. Now, that is a very long cruise which took over 30 days to complete. It took that length of time because our ship was old and could not travel greater than a speed of sixteen knots.

My best friend on the ship was Ben Pruitt. Ben was the chief quartermaster and his job was to make sure that the ship kept on its course and ended up at its intended destination. Chief Quartermaster Pruitt was very accomplished at his job, having logged almost twenty years at sea as a US Navy Quartermaster. I was a young electronics technician about to turn twenty years of age, and very inquisitive about everything.

Most every evening Ben and I would travel up to the highest deck on the Seminole, and with his sexton he would "shoot the stars" to determine our exact location. There were no satellites in those days to provide guidance. Invariably, the ship was a little off course and would have to make a correction. This process was called "keeping the stars." It meant that our intent was to keep on course by "keeping to the stars".

The same is true with "keeping the commandments." It is our intent to keep God's commandments, but we often stray off course. We must get back on the narrow way to our destination by confessing our sins and correcting the course of our lives.

It is therefore the intent of our heart that matters. Our intent must be to keep His commandments.

Bear God's fruit

Matthew 7:16-20; 15:15-20; 12:33-35; Mark 7:20-23; John 15:1-11, 16; 21:15-17; James 2:14-26; II Peter 1:5-11; III John 1:11; Galatians 5:22-23 (Some verses for further study.)

Some key verses:

"You will know them by their fruits. Grapes are not gathered from thorn bushes, nor figs from thistles, are they? Even so, every good tree bears good fruit; but the rotten tree bears bad fruit.

A good tree cannot produce bad fruit, nor can a rotten tree produce good fruit. Every tree that does not bear good fruit is cut down and thrown into the fire. So then, you will know them by their fruits." Matthew 7:16

"By this is My Father glorified, that you bear much fruit, and so prove to be My disciples." John 15:8

"Now for this very reason also, applying all diligence, in your faith supply moral excellence, and in your moral excellence, knowledge; and in your knowledge, self-control, and in your self-control, perseverance, and in your perseverance, godliness; and in your godliness, brotherly kindness, and in your brotherly kindness, Christian love. For if these qualities are yours and are increasing, they render you neither useless nor unfruitful in the true knowledge of our Lord Jesus Christ. For he who lacks these qualities is blind or short-sighted, having forgotten his purification from his former sins. Therefore, brethren, be all the more diligent to make certain about His calling and choosing you; for as long as you practice these things, you will never stumble; for in this way the entrance into the eternal kingdom of our Lord and Savior Jesus Christ will be abundantly supplied to you." II Peter 1:5-11

What about this fruit bearing thing?

- Is it service for the Lord? No.
- Is it attending church or praying? No.
- Is it money we have given? No.
- Is it sermons preached or souls won? No.

These things may overflow out of fruit, but they are not what the Bible means when talking about "bearing fruit."

If you plant an apple seed, you get an apple tree which bears apples. If you plant a watermelon seed, you get watermelons; orange seeds, oranges; and so on.

The fruit is determined by the nature of the seed. If the seed of God's Word and the Holy Spirit is planted in us, we will bear the fruit of the Holy Spirit. Which Paul defines as quoted above in Galatians 5:22. Good fruit produced by the Spirit but evident in the life of a believer.

The bad fruit Paul earlier defined as:

"Now the works of the flesh are evident, which are adultery, fornication, uncleanness, lewdness, idolatry, sorcery, hatred, contentions, jealousies, outbursts of wrath, selfish ambitions, dissensions, heresies, envy, murders, drunkenness, revelries and the like ... those who practice such things will not inherit the kingdom of God." Galatians 5:19-21

Yeshua said in Matthew Chapter Seven:

"Enter by the narrow gate, for wide is the gate and broad is the way that leads to destruction, and there are many who go in by it. Because narrow is the gate and difficult is the way which leads to life, and there are few who find it." (vv. 13 &14)

"Not everyone who says to me "Lord, Lord shall enter the kingdom but he who does the will of My Father in heaven. Many will say to me in that day, Lord, Lord, have we not prophesied in Your name, cast out demons in Your name, and done many wonders in Your name?

And then I will declare to them, I never knew you, depart from Me you who practice lawlessness?" (vv. 21 – 23)

When Yeshua raptures His Church, many will be "left behind", as my friend Tim LaHaye wrote in his books by that name before he went to heaven.

Many will be left who thought they were going to the marriage feast of the Lamb (Revelations 19:9) only to be locked out.

To paraphrase what Jesus said:

Those left behind will say things like "did we not pray a prayer to accept you when we were young, did we not teach Sunday school and vacation bible school, did we not tithe, serve as deacons, preach sermons, stop smoking and drinking?" And He will say "I never knew you. Depart from Me."

Recently a gifted young Pastor of a sizable church in South Georgia told the following story during his Sunday morning message.

A man and his wife had decided to escape the cold wintery weather of Northern Michigan, for a two week vacation in Miami, Florida. As they were preparing to leave the wife was summoned into an important Board meeting. She would need to delay her departure for a day. The husband went as scheduled.

Arriving in Miami and after getting settled into his hotel room the man decided to email his wife to let her know he had arrived safely. He pulled out his phone and typed in a message, but he had to guess at his wife's email address. He pressed send and the message went through.

Meanwhile, back in North Carolina a pastor's wife was preparing to bury her husband. The Pastor had just passed away and the family was all gathered together to plan for the funeral and memorial service. The Pastor and his wife had served faithfully for many years at the local Southern Baptist Church.

The pastor's son hurriedly brought his mom's cell phone to her, which had just received what looked like an important message. The Pastor's wife read the message, screamed loudly, and immediately fainted.

Confused, the son picked up the phone and read the message.

"To my wonderful wife. I have just checked in and wanted to let you know that everything is prepared for your arrival tomorrow. One thing, it is really hot down here. Your loving husband."

The Michigan man had apparently sent his email to the wrong email address.

I suspect that when we face Jesus and He says to some *"I never knew you, depart from me" (Matthew 7:23)* there will be much screaming and fainting.

So who is on the narrow path to enter thru the narrow gate?

Those who have accepted Yeshua as their Lord and Savior, repented of their sin, confessed Him as Lord of their lives, AND their lives reflect Jesus by their attitude toward the things of the world, they are "keeping the commandments" and bearing the good fruit of the Spirit. All others are on the wide path and will be left behind.

As the apostle James puts it:

"Therefore lay aside all filthiness and overflow of wickedness, and receive with meekness the implanted Word (seed), which is able to save your souls. But be doers of the word, and not hearers only, deceiving yourselves." James 1:21&22

All three of these evidences (attitude toward the world, keeping the commandments and bearing fruit) of our love for God and of our being participants in His plan are summarized in an encounter between Jesus and Peter at the Sea of Galilee, after Christ's resurrection.

"So when they had finished breakfast, Jesus said to Simon Peter, "Simon, son of John, do you love Me more than these?" He said to Him, "Yes, Lord; You know that I love You." He said to him, "Tend My lambs."

He said to him again a second time, "Simon, son of John, do you love Me?" He said to Him, "Yes, Lord; You know that I love You." He said to him, "Shepherd My sheep."

He said to him the third time, "Simon, son of John, do you love Me?" And he said to Him, "Lord, You know all things; You know that I love You." Jesus said to him, "Tend My sheep." John 21:15-17

Do you love God? Do you have His attitude toward the things of the world? Are you following His precepts and does your life produce God's fruit? How are you sharing the gospel and ministering to God's sheep?

Are you a participant in God's plan? Those who have the Holy Spirit are participants with God in His plan, those who do not have the Holy Spirit are not participants.

It's that simple.

If you find that you are not a participant in God's plan I urge you to take the first step and accept Him as your Lord and Savior. Trust in Jesus Christ alone for your salvation.

If you are not a Christian this is the most important message contained in this book.

We make a living by what we get; we make a life by what we give. — Winston Churchill

STEWARDSHIP - THE PRINCIPLES

As I wrote earlier, a **principle** can be thought of as the reason behind a precept. The fundamental truth upon which a precept is based. Now we are going to explore some Biblical principles related to stewardship.

The ultimate truth in all creation is of course, God. He is the corner stone of life. The source from which all of life emanates. Any principle, or "fundamental truth," must come from this "corner stone" (God), and must always point toward Him.

Principles are not the base of the column of life, but they are the capital of it. Principles are not given as a way to obtain life, but as the way in which to exhibit life. The base of the column is God's foundational truths.

Foundational Truths

Therefore, before we begin our study of God's "fundamental truths," His principles, it is important that we define the person of God and agree on certain truths about God, which I believe to be foundational to any understanding or application of God's plan.

1. The Bible is God's inerrant Word

2. God created all things and is sovereign over all things

3. God is the Father, the Son and the Holy Spirit

4. God is Savior

5. God can be described with the qualities of deity, power and moral character.

Qualities of Deity:

God was not created. He was always there. He exists forever. He is always the same.

>   *SELF-EXISTENCE:* Romans 1:23; I Timothy 6:16
>   *INFINITY:* Isaiah 48:12; Psalm 90:2; Psalm 102:26-27
>   *ETERNITY:* Psalm 93:2; Jeremiah 10:10

Qualities of Power:

God is all powerful, has infinite knowledge and is present in all places at the same time.

>   *OMNIPOTENCE:* II Samuel 22:33; Matthew 28:18;
>   *OMNISCIENCE:* Job 37:14-16; John 21:17
>   *OMNIPRESENCE:* Ephesians 4:10

Qualities of Moral Character:

>   *HOLY:* Isaiah 6:3; John 17:11; Hebrews 7:26-28; I Peter 1:16; Psalms 99:5; Psalms 99:9; I Samuel 2:2; Isaiah 43:3: *"For I am the Lord your God, The Holy One of Israel, your Savior;"* Isaiah 43:15:*"I am the Lord, your Holy One, The Creator of Israel, your King."*

>   *LOVE:* Exodus 34:6-7; John 3:16; *"The one who does not love does not know God, for God is love. By this the love of God was manifested in us, that God has sent His only begotten Son into the world so that we might live through Him. In this is love, not that we loved God, but that He loved us and sent His Son to be the propitiation for our sins."* I John 4:8-10

>   *TRUTH:* II Samuel 7:28; Psalms 31:5 and 119:160; Isaiah 65:16; Romans 3:4; *"Sanctify them in the truth; Thy word is truth."* John 17:17

MERCY: *"It is because of the Lord's mercies that we are not consumed, because his compassions fail not. They are new every morning; great is thy faithfulness."* Lamentations 3:22-23 KJV

FAITHFULNESS: Psalms 36:5 and 119:90; Lamentations 3:23; Romans 8:32; *"Let us hold fast the confession of our hope without wavering, for He who promised is faithful."* Hebrews 10:23

GOODNESS: Romans 11:22; *"For how great is His goodness, and how great is his beauty!"* Zechariah 9:17

PATIENCE: Exodus 34:6-7; *"Now the God of patience and consolation grant you to be like-minded one toward another according to Christ Jesus, that ye may with one mind and   one mouth glorify God, even the Father of our Lord Jesus Christ."* Romans 15:5

JUSTICE: Genesis 18:25; Psalms 75:7; Hebrews 12:23; *"Which of the prophets have not your fathers persecuted? And they have   slain them who showed before of the coming of the Just One, of whom ye have been now the betrayers and murderers."* Acts 7:52 KJV

God established absolute moral standards.

Now, this statement may seem naïve and perhaps even silly to the intellectual non-Christian. It may be that some who call themselves Christian even think this is a bit over-board and they agree intellectually with the non-believer, thus denying the authority of scripture. The world tells us that there are no absolutes ... no absolute truth and no absolute morals.

The Christian's faith must be in God and God alone. Our intellect, rational arguments, or someone else's intellect falls far short of God. Believing God's Word and following His precepts is not intellectual suicide.

Theories of science and philosophies are constantly changing. Placing belief in a proven perfect and unchanging God instead of a proven imperfect and ever changing secular philosophy seems very rational to me. God established absolute moral standards and absolute truth.

As Dr. A. W. Tozer wrote so well in his classic book _The Knowledge of The Holy_:

"The divine attributes are what we know to be true of God. He does not possess them as qualities; they are how God is as He reveals Himself to His creatures. Love, for instance, is not something God has and which may grow or diminish or cease to be. His love in the way God is, and when He loves He is simply being Himself. And so with the other attributes. "

"Between His attributes no contradiction can exist. He need not suspend one to exercise another, for in Him all His attributes are one. All of God does all that God does; He does not divide Himself to perform a work, but works in the total of His being."[iv]

God created mankind in His "image."

"Then God said, "Let Us make man in Our image, according to Our likeness; and let them rule over the fish of the sea and over the birds of the sky and over the cattle and over all the earth, and over every creeping thing that creeps on the earth."

"And God created man in His own image, in the image of God He created him; male and female He created them." Gen. 1:26-27

By this I think we were created as free spiritual beings with the power of choice, with the ability to communicate with God, and with the qualities of God's moral character. Through sin we lost the moral qualities of this "image" of God and it can only be regained through acceptance of His Son and the indwelling of His Spirit. This is what God means when Paul wrote 2 Corinthians 3:18:

"But we all, with unveiled face, beholding as in a mirror the glory of the Lord, are being transformed into the same image from glory to glory, just as from the Lord, the Spirit."

As Christians we see God in His Son and demonstrated by His moral character. *"When I was a child, I used to speak as a child, think as a child, reason as a child; when I became a man, I did away with childish things. For now we see in a mirror dimly, but then face to face; now I know in part, but then I shall know fully just as I also have been fully known."* I Corinthians 13:11-12.

We are therefore to increasingly reflect His qualities of moral character. This is accomplished through the work of the Holy Spirit in our lives. *"But the fruit of the Spirit is love, joy, peace, patience, kindness, goodness, self-control; against such things there is no law."* Galatians 5:22-23.

As Christians we are told to put on the likeness of God - His moral character.

"But you did not learn Christ in this way, if indeed you have heard Him and have been taught in Him, just as truth is in Jesus, that, in reference to your former manner of life, you lay aside the old self, which is being corrupted in accordance with the lusts of deceit, and that you be renewed in the spirit of your mind, and put on the new self, which in the likeness of God has been created in righteousness and holiness of the truth." Ephesians 4:20-24.

As Christians we are told to be imitators of God - His moral character. *"Therefore be imitators of God, as beloved children."* Ephesians 5:1

And finally, as Christians we are told to put on the new self which is in the image of our Creator. *"Do not lie to one another, since you laid aside the old self with its evil practices, and have put on the new self who is being renewed to a true knowledge according to the image of the One who created him, - a renewal in which there is no distinction between Greek and Jew, circumcised and uncircumcised, barbarian, Scythian, slave and freeman, but Christ is all and in all."* Colossians 3:9-11.

Now to the principles.

THE PRINCIPLE OF OWNERSHIP

Webster's New World Dictionary defines a steward as *"one who acts as a supervisor or administrator, as of finances and property, for another."* We are therefore administrators of God's property while we are alive on earth. We own nothing. He entrusts us with varying amounts of His property as He determines.

As Christians we must adopt and maintain God's view of life and of the world. In other words, God's Word and Jesus Christ must be our paradigm or the glasses through which we view all of life including work, business, our personal wealth and finances. God has much to say about stewardship.

How do you define wealth? Is it money? Currency has no intrinsic value but merely derives its worth by society assigning a representative value to it. It is worth the goods and services for which it can be traded. Are these goods and services therefore earthly wealth? Yes, but I believe God's concept of wealth is far greater than this; in fact, goods and services do not top God's list of wealth.

Certainly Jesus valued God's Word and the worship of God above bread, when he was starving and above all the kingdoms of the world when he had no possessions (Matthew 4:1-11).

God gives us other glimpses of His concept of true wealth.

"Happy is the person who finds wisdom and gains understanding. For the profit of wisdom is better than silver, and her wages are better than gold. Wisdom is more precious than rubies; nothing you desire can compare with her. She offers you life in her right hand, and riches and honor in her left." Proverbs 3:13-16

*"A worthy wife is her husband's joy and crown..."*Proverbs 12:4a
"Who can find a virtuous and capable wife? She is worth more than precious rubies." Proverbs 31:10

"Choose a good reputation over great riches, for being held in high esteem is better than having silver or gold." Proverbs 22:1

Therefore wealth, is what money can buy, but more, much more. It is God's Word, wisdom, knowledge, abilities, skills, talents, spiritual gifts, a good name and reputation, family, health, personality, appearance, heritage, friends, culture, circumstances, opportunity, and even our very thoughts and ideas. It is everything created by God and entrusted to us.

It is important to understand that all wealth, however you define it, is from God.

- o **NATURAL RESOURCES** ... (Genesis 1)

- o **HUMAN TRAITS AND ABILITIES** ... (1 Corinthians 4:7)

- o **CIRCUMSTANCES** ... (Haggai 1:11)

It's all God's property

"I have no complaint about your sacrifices or the burnt offerings you constantly bring to my altar. But I want no more bulls from your barns; I want no more goats from your pens. For all the animals of the forest are mine, and I own the cattle on a thousand hills. Every bird of the mountains and all the animals of the field belong to me. If I were hungry, I would not mention it to you, for all the world is mine and everything in it." Psalms 50:8-12

"He is the God who made the world and everything in it. Since he is Lord of heaven and earth, he doesn't live in man-made temples, and human hands can't serve his needs-for he has no needs. He himself gives life and breath to everything, and he satisfies every need there is. From one man he created all the nations throughout the whole earth. He decided beforehand which should rise and fall, and he determined their boundaries. His purpose in all of this was that the nations should seek after God and perhaps feel their way toward him and find him-though he is not far from any one of us. For in him we live and move and exist. As one of your own poets says, 'We are his offspring.'" Acts 17:24-28

I've found few better examples of someone living the Biblical principle of God's ownership than R. Stanley Tam. Stanley spoke to my class at California Baptist University about stewardship.

In 1969 Mr. Tam wrote a book chronicling his experiences of adhering to this principle entitled "God Owns My Business." It's the story of his life.

Stanly Tam grew up as a poor, shy, Ohio farm boy during the 1920s. He began work peddling household items door-to-door. At the writing of his book, his businesses had become large and profitable, donating well over a million dollars annually, a significant sum in 1969.

He had however, transferred the actual ownership of these businesses to a non-profit corporation. The mission of the non-profit corporation was to donate funds for Christian work.

Why did Stanly do this? The answer in his own words:

"In over 47 years of business life I have found Christ to be the source of all my needs. Every time He takes me through a valley He brings me out stronger, wiser and more dependent upon Him. My love and devotion for Him grow each year.

He gives me a purpose for which to Live. ...My prime effort in life is to be obedient to my God, to serve Him and bring credit to His name. ...And so on January 15, 1955, I told God I would no longer be a stockholder in either States Smelting and Refining Corporation or the United States Plastic Corporation. All stock would belong to Him. I would be merely an employee."v

How did Stanley get to this point of stewardship in his life? Let me describe an incident in Mr. Tam's early business career that will give a partial answer to this question. For the complete answer read his book.

Stanley Tam had gotten into the silver reclamation business through the help of an inventor whom Stanley called Mr. Aukerman. By 1932 Eastman Kodak Company was consuming nearly 20 tons of silver weekly in the production of its film. Eighty percent of this silver was washed off and sent down the drain in the process of developing prints from exposed negatives.

Mr. Aukerman had developed a product that would capture this silver during the developing process. It could then be resold to Kodak. Stanley read of the invention and Mr. Aukerman, tracked him down and entered into an agreement to manufacture and market the invention.

This was the beginning of his business. By 1943 the original invention was proving to be less efficient than needed. Mr. Aukerman had developed a greatly improved version. Tam again eagerly contracted to manufacture and sell the new product. *"The contract specified that I was to pay him royalties, that I was not to question his patent, and that if I ever quit using collectors, I was to turn my records over to him so he could service the customers."[vi]*

By 1945 Stanley Tam discovered that Mr. Aukerman's patent on the new silver collector was faulty. The silver collector was public domain, so anyone could manufacture and sell the identical product.

Stanley consulted an attorney who advised him to pay Mr. Aukerman no more royalties. Stanley took the advice. His business continued to boom despite not having the exclusive rights to the product. Three years passed and Stanley Tam was busy spearheading an evangelistic crusade in his home city of Lima, Ohio.

"And then God began speaking to me! "Stanley, how can you pray for revival when all is not right is your own life? Look at the way you have treated that inventor." "Lord," I prayed silently, "we're not praying for Mr. Aukerman tonight. We're praying for our city-wide evangelistic crusade." But the voice of God was persistent.

"You signed a contract with Mr. Aukerman. You agreed to pay him royalty, and you agreed not to question the patent. Do you know you perpetrated falsehood when you went to the attorney and questioned the patent?" "But maybe that's why he put the clause in the contract," I argued. "He knew the patent was faulty. Can't I stand on my rights as a citizen?"

"There are two kinds of laws, Stanley. There is man's law, and there is My law.

You could drink a quart of whiskey tonight and not break any law in the state of Ohio, but you would break My law. By whose standard are you living, man's or Mine?"[vii]

Stanley contacted Mr. Aukerman, explained his convictions and, much to the surprise of Mr. Aukerman and Mr. Aukerman's daughter, agreed to pay for the patent.

"An enormous load rolled off my heart as we signed that agreement. Not only had things been put right between myself and Mr. Aukerman, but also the clogged channels were cleared between myself and my Lord.

In December of that year Mr. Aukerman suffered a sudden cerebral hemorrhage, was unconscious for two weeks, and died a few days after Christmas. When I received the letter telling of his death, I buried my face in my hands. "Dear God," I prayed, "what if I had delayed obeying You? He could have one day stood before Your judgement throne and accused a hypocrite of standing in his way."

"Aukerman's daughter wrote: He had his picture taken just after you were here and asked me to send one to you. But then he took suddenly ill, and I didn't get it attended to. It is enclosed." It was my subsequent privilege to be a guest in this woman's Wilmington home. She now has a personal and vital faith in Christ. Do you wonder why?"[viii]

Stanley recognized God's ownership and followed God's principle of stewardship rather than to stand on his rights. God blessed him as He promised He would.

This experience, built upon other such experiences, led Stanley Tam to transfer complete ownership of himself to God. After that, turning over the ownership of his businesses was natural.

This is the fundamental principle of biblical stewardship: God owns everything and we are simply the managers, we own nothing.

"You may say to yourself, 'My power and the strength of my hands have produced this wealth for me.' But remember the Lord your God, for it is he who gives you the ability to produce wealth." Deuteronomy 8:17 & 18

It is all God's.

THE PRINCIPLE OF ATTITUDE

Our attitude toward the things of this world is critical to becoming God's steward.

> *"Don't store up treasures here on earth, where they can be eaten by moths and get rusty, and where thieves break in and steal. Store your treasures in heaven, where they will never become moth-eaten or rusty and where they will be safe from thieves.* **Wherever your treasure is, there your heart and thoughts will also be.***"* Matthew 6:19-21

> *"No one can serve two masters. For you will hate one and love the other, or be devoted to one and despise the other.* **You cannot serve both God and money.***"* Luke 16:13

> *"Stop loving this evil world and all that it offers you, for when you love the world, you show that you do not have the love of the Father in you.*
>
> *For the world offers only the lust for physical pleasure, the lust for everything we see, and pride in our possessions. These are not from the Father. They are from this evil world."* 1 John 2:15-16

> *"And even when you do ask, you don't get it because your whole motive is wrong-you want only what will give you pleasure."* James 4:3

> *"Stay away from the love of money; be satisfied with what you have. For God has said, 'I will never fail you. I will never forsake you.'"* Hebrews 13:5

We can't deceive God concerning our attitude

> *"There was no poverty among them, because people who owned land or houses sold them and brought the money to the apostles to give to others in need...There was also a man named Ananias who, with his wife, Sapphira, sold some property. He brought part of the money to the apostles, but he claimed it was the full amount. His wife had agreed to this deception. Then Peter said, 'Ananias, why has Satan filled your heart? You lied to the Holy Spirit, and you kept some of the money for yourself. The property was yours to sell or not sell, as you wished. And after selling it, the money was yours to give away. How could you do a thing like this? You weren't lying to us but to God.' As soon as Ananias heard these words, he fell to the floor and died. Everyone who heard about it was terrified."* Acts 4:34-35, 5:1-5

God dealt forcefully and swiftly with deceit as an example to the early Church. Our attitude is important to God. I will write more about attitude a little later.

THE PRINCIPLE OF OBLIGATION

People will rightfully infer from us a picture of the Master if we claim to represent Him. We are His reflections. Therefore, we are to represent Him well. This does not mean that we are required to be highly successful, renowned, wealthy or exceptionally brilliant people? No, we are but to follow His principles and precepts without compromise and seek to glorify Him. These are our obligations as stewards:

- o **KNOW WHO THE MASTER IS.**

- o **KNOW THE MASTER'S DESIRES.**

- o **REPRESENT THE MASTER WELL.**

"Who is a faithful, sensible servant, to whom the master can give the responsibility of managing his household and feeding his family? If the master returns and finds that the servant has done a good job, there will be a reward." Matthew 24:45-46

God wanted us, as His reflections, to first reveal our love to Him by our right attitude toward things, and second to be successful in our stewardship over these things. In so doing we glorify Him and make Him known to others.

First, He instructs us as to our attitude toward possessions.

Second, He instructs us as to our administration, or stewardship over these possessions.

Third, He instructs us as to how to reflect God's character through our lives and our work.

These instructions: God's **Biblical principles,** and His **Biblical precepts**, all point to His **Person**.

Please keep in mind that we are not to adhere to God's principles or precepts in order to be saved but because we are saved. Therefore we have God's nature in us, He is able to conform us to His image.

God does not need our help nor our gifts to bring about His plan for the world. The good news for us is that God has chosen to work with and through us as we have faith and are obedient to Him.

THE PRINCIPLE OF FREEDOM

To give is a choice, a freedom, and a decision every person must make in their own hearts.

Even the word, "give" communicates that people are not under a command to distribute their resources. God in His wisdom, under the New Covenant of Jesus Christ, entrusted His children to respond according to their heart's desire. True freedom!

At the same time, the desires of our hearts are what catch the attention of God. One day, Jesus was watching people as they gave at temple.

> *"Jesus sat down near the collection box in the Temple and watched as the crowds dropped in their money. Many rich people put in large amounts.*
>
> *Then a poor widow came and dropped in two small coins. Jesus called His disciples to Him and said, "I tell you the truth, this poor widow has given more than all the others who are making contributions."* Mark 12:41-43

Jesus and the disciples observed many people bringing their gifts to the temple. What is most interesting about this story is not what people gave, but the fact that Jesus watched.

And what Jesus watched and saw with His eyes was not what man sees. Jesus was able to see the hearts of the people.

It wasn't their money; it was their *hearts* that caught His eye. Afterward, Jesus called together His disciples and talked about what they observed.

He pointed out that this humble widow gave more, not in monetary terms, but considerably more in terms of her heart.

We have the freedom to give, as the widow gave, from our hearts.

THE PRINCIPLE OF OBEDIENCE

Once we discover what it is that God wants us to do it may become frightening to trust Him enough to actually do it.

The story is told about a man, let's call him Bill, who was walking along a steep cliff late one evening. It had been raining and the ground was wet and slippery. Bill was an experienced hiker, but he never should have been walking along the cliff in these conditions.

Then it happened. He accidentally got too close to the edge and slipped off the cliff. While falling he somehow managed to grab a tree root which was growing out of the cliff side. This temporarily stopped his fall. He looked down and to his horror saw that the canyon fell straight down as far as he could see. To fall would mean certain death. The sides of the cliff were wet and slippery and Bill could not get any foothold to even attempt to climb back up. He couldn't hang onto the root forever

Out of desperation he began yelling for help, hoping beyond hope that someone passing by would hear him and help him up. However at this time of the day, there were no other hikers as irresponsible as he had been. "HELP! HELP!" He yelled for a long time as loud as he could, but no one answered him. He was about to give up yelling when he heard a voice.

"Bill, Bill. Can you hear me?" "Yes, yes! I can hear you. I'm down here but who and where are you!"

"I am God. Bill, I'm here."

"God, please help me! I promise, if you'll get me up from here, I'll serve You for the rest of my life."

"Hold up on the promises, Bill. Let's first get you back onto solid ground, then we can talk. Now, here is what I want you to do. Pay very close attention."

"I'll do anything you ask, God. Just tell me what to do."

"Turn loose of the root."

"What?!"

"I said, let go of the root. Trust Me Bill, let it go."

There was a long silence.

Finally Bill yelled, "Help, Help, is anyone else up there?"[ix]

When we discover what it is that God wants us to do, or to give, or to be, it is sometimes frightening to take that first step and actually do what we know should be done. To actually turn loose of the root.

Of course this was a made-up story about Bill to make a point. However, the first book of Kings, Chapter seventeen relates the account of Elijah and gives the true story of his encounter with a widow from Zarephath.

God was withholding rain from Israel in judgment of the nation's idolatry, led by Ahab and Jezebel. No rain or even dew. There was great famine in the land. Amid this condition God then commanded Elijah to go to Zarephath, where a widow would provide food for him. Elijah obeyed, finding a woman gathering sticks. He said to her, "Bring me a little water in a vessel, that I may drink," and, "Bring me a morsel of bread in your hand."

The widow, however, was in great need herself. She responded, "As the Lord your God lives, I have nothing baked, only a handful of flour in a jar and a little oil in a jug. And now I am gathering a couple of sticks that I may go in and prepare it for myself and my son that we may eat it and die".

Elijah told her that she was to make some food for him, using the last of her ingredients for his consumption. He added a promise: "For thus says the Lord, the God of Israel, 'The jar of flour shall not be spent, and the jug of oil shall not be empty, until the day that the Lord sends rain upon the earth".

In other words, "Let go of the root." The widow's faith was evident in her obedience. And God was faithful to His promise:

"She and he and her household ate for many days. The jar of flour was not spent, neither did the jug of oil become empty, according to the word of the Lord that he spoke by Elijah". I Kings 17:15&16

The widow's food and oil were miraculously extended, as promised.

The principle of obedience demonstrated in the lives of Elijah and the widow.

THE PRINCIPLE OF UNITY

"United we stand, divided we fall". *Aesop*

I served four years in the US Navy, and three years were spent in Viet Nam. Two of those three years were aboard an Attack Cargo Ship landing marines and supplies onto the shores, and the last year was with Special Forces, Beach Jumper Unit One. In both situations we were trained to act as a unit. Each person did his job, but it was one unit and one mission. The strength was in the unified action. There is strength in unity.

We can see a picture of strength when the Christians unite shortly after Pentecost as recorded in the book of Acts. When believers unify the result is victory.

"Now the multitude of those who believed were of one heart and one soul: neither did anyone say that any of the things he possessed was his own, but they had all things in common. And with great power the apostles gave witness to the resurrection of the Lord Jesus. And great grace was upon them all." Acts 4: 32 & 33

A modern day example of victory in unity is the Southern Baptist Convention. A collection of thousands of independent churches, and millions of believers coming together as a unit to reach the world for Christ. The following information is from the SBC website http://www.sbc.net:

The Southern Baptist Convention (SBC) is a fellowship of over 47,000 Baptist churches scattered across the United States and its territories. These congregations, comprised of numerous racial, ethnic, language, and socioeconomic people groups, are called "cooperating churches." They have organized themselves to accomplish a specific set of missions and ministry initiatives, all for the purpose of proclaiming the Gospel of Jesus Christ to all people everywhere.

Cooperating Churches	47,456
Total membership in the SBC network of churches	14,813,234
Weekly worship attendance	5,297,788
Total baptisms reported by Southern Baptist churches	246,442
Cooperating state conventions	41

God gives each believer certain gifts and the believer is supposed to use those gifts in a unified effort together with other believers to spread the Gospel and glorify the Lord. One body, one cause but diverse talents. 1 Corinthians 12: 4 – 20:

"There are diversities of gifts, but the same Spirit. There are differences of ministries, but the same Lord. And there are diversities of activities, but it is the same God who works all in all.

But the manifestation of the Spirit is given to each one for the profit of all: for to one is given the word of wisdom through the Spirit, to another the word of knowledge through the same Spirit, to another faith by the same Spirit, to another gifts of healings by the same Spirit, to another the working of miracles, to another prophecy, to another discerning of spirits, to another different kinds of tongues, to another the interpretation of tongues. But one and the same Spirit works all these things, distributing to each one individually as He wills.

For as the body is one and has many members, but all the members of that one body, being many, are one body, so also is Christ. For by one Spirit we were all baptized into one body — whether Jews or Greeks, whether slaves or free — and have all been made to drink into one Spirit.

For in fact the body is not one member but many. If the foot should say, "Because I am not a hand, I am not of the body," is it therefore not of the body? And if the ear should say, "Because I am not an eye, I am not of the body," is it therefore not of the body? If the whole body were an eye, where would be the hearing? If the whole were hearing, where would be the smelling?

But now God has set the members, each one of them, in the body just as He pleased. And if they were all one member, where would the body be? But now indeed there are many members, yet one body. "

Therefore one essential principle of stewardship is the strong message that God gave us, that every individual Christian believer has their own unique gift(s) to perform their own unique task(s) in the world. No one individual can do everything, but each must do what God has created them to do. This limiting by God means that He wants the whole of His church to work together for the accomplishing of His will.

Each and every born again believer was given the task of being God's steward.

GOD'S HARVEST PRINCIPLE

This principle can be best illustrated through the farming world of sowing and reaping. What a man sows so shall he reap.

"Do not be deceived, God is not mocked, for whatever a man sows, that he will also reap. For he who sows to his flesh will of the flesh reap corruption, but he who sows to the Spirit will of the Spirit reap everlasting life. And let us not grow weary while doing good, for in due season we shall reap if we do not lose heart." Galatians 6: 7-9

As discussed earlier, if you plant an apple seed you get apples, and if you plant a kernel of corn you will get corn. The nature of the harvest is determined by the nature of the seed. If you plant the Spirit of God you will reap everlasting life.

The harvest principle is best explained through the examination of the precepts pointing to this principle, which we will look at closely in the next chapter.

To summarize. The seven principles of Biblical stewardship:

1. The principle of ownership
2. The principle of attitude
3. The principle of obligation
4. The principle of freedom
5. The principle of obedience
6. The principle of unity.
7. The harvest principle.

I was once young and now I am old, but not once have I been witness to God's failure to supply my need when first I had given for the furtherance of His work. He has never failed in His promise, so I cannot fail in my service to Him. — William Carey

STEWARDSHIP – THE PRECEPTS

Let us now explore God's precepts of stewardship. As defined earlier, rules of conduct which point us to God's principles of stewardship.

God's Word gives the precepts supporting God's Harvest Principle (as taught to me by Pastor David Jeremiah, and also included in his booklet, _Giving in the Grace Zone_, page 45):

A.   The **PRECEPT OF INVESTMENT** – John 12:24

We reap only **IF** we sow.

> _"Most assuredly, I say to you, unless a grain of wheat falls into the ground and dies, it remains alone, but if it dies, it produces much grain"._

Simply put, if we don't sow, we won't reap.

Consider this example: One kernel of corn contains all the potential to reproduce. If I plant the kernel, it will reproduce itself and bring forth many times the original kernel – each new kernel containing the potential to be planted and yield even more kernels.

That cycle can go on and on producing countless millions of kernels. However, if I take that kernel of corn and cherish it and put it into a frame or jar on my desk so that I can admire it and show it off, it will never grow or multiply. The only way that kernel of corn can be valuable and obtain its created potential is if it is planted or invested. As long as I hold onto the things God has given me, refusing to sow them back into the harvest field, I will never see any increase.

The precept of **INVESTMENT** – We reap only if we sow.

B.   The **PRECEPT OF IDENTITY** – Galatians 6:8

We reap only **WHAT** we sow.

"Those who live only to satisfy their own sinful desires will harvest the consequences of decay and death. But those who live to please the Spirit will harvest everlasting life from the Spirit."

If I plant corn, then I will harvest corn. I cannot plant corn and expect to harvest watermelon. I will harvest whatever I plant. In other words – we reap exactly what we sow. If I sow anger and discord, my life will be filled with anger and discord. The only way to have friends is to sow friendship.

The precept of **IDENTITY** – We reap only what we sow.

C.   The **PRECEPT OF INCREASE** – 2 Corinthians 9: 6&10

We reap **MORE** than we sow.

"Remember this--a farmer who plants only a few seeds will get a small crop. But the one who plants generously will get a generous crop."

"For God is the one who gives seed to the farmer and then bread to eat. In the same way, he will give you many opportunities to do good, and he will produce a great harvest of generosity in you."

If I planted a kernel of corn, nourished it, waited six months, and harvested only one kernel of corn, there would be no reason to sow.

There is no gain if there is no increase. But that is not how it works. God has arranged for things to grow and to multiply if we invest them. We always get only what we sow and we always get more than we sow.

In explaining this concept to the Corinthian believer, Paul used the Greek word for abundance five times in this passage:

> "And God is able to make all grace **abound** toward you, that you, **always** having **all sufficiency** in all things may have an **abundance** for **every** good work."
> II Corinthians 9:8

What kind of multiplier does God use when creating His return?

Matthew 19:29 "...shall receive a hundredfold"

This is a 10,000 percent return!

The precept of INCREASE – we reap more than we sow.

D.   The **PRECEPT OF INTERVAL** – Galatians 6:9

We reap **LATER** than we sow.

"So don't get tired of doing what is good. Don't get discouraged and give up, for we will reap a harvest of blessing at the appropriate time."

When I plant I must wait for the harvest. If I plant corn one day, I cannot expect to harvest more corn the next day. No matter how anxious or upset I become, I cannot harvest the corn until the proper time. It takes time for a crop to grow into maturity.

"So, my dear brothers and sisters, be strong and immovable. Always work enthusiastically for the Lord, for you know that nothing you do for the Lord is ever useless." I Corinthians 15:58

The precept of INTERVAL – we reap later than we sow.

THE PRECEPT – BLOOM WHERE GOD PLANTS YOU

When our family set out to be missionaries to Peru, someone gave my wife a throw-pillow onto which was sewn the words "Bloom Where You Are Planted". Sounds Biblical doesn't it? However there is no such phrase in the Bible. You can search your concordance until the cows come home, but you will not find the words "Bloom where you are planted". It is simply not in the Bible, anywhere. I know. I searched.

There are other colloquial phrases that we use that are often mistaken as biblical statements. "Spare the rod and spoil the child", "Cleanliness is next to godliness", "God moves in mysterious ways". All of these sound Biblical but are simply not in the Bible.

The question we really need to ask ourselves is what does it mean? And is this meaning or concept found in God's Word.

It seems to me that the phrase "Bloom where you are planted" means that we are to be content where God has placed us, and we are to make the most of our particular circumstances for the Glory of God.

This concept is found in the Word. 1 Corinthians 7:20 – 24:

"Let each one remain in the same calling in which he was called. Were you called while a slave?

Do not be concerned about it; but if you can be made free rather use it. For he who is called in the Lord while a slave is the Lord's freeman.

Likewise he who is called while free is Christ's slave. You were bought at a price, do not become slaves of men. Brethren, let each one remain with God in that state in which he was called."

John Calvin wrote,

"Finally, this point is to be noted: the Lord bids each one of us in all life's actions to look to his calling. For he knows with what great restlessness human nature flames, with what fickleness is borne hither and thither, how its ambition longs to embrace various things at once.

Therefore, lest through our stupidity and rashness everything be turned topsy-turvy, he has appointed duties for every man in his particular way of life. And that no one may thoughtlessly transgress his limits, he has named the various kinds of living "callings."

Therefore each individual has his own kind of living assigned to him by the Lord as a sort of sentry post so that he may not heedlessly wander about throughout life." (*Institutes*, 3.10.6).

Bloom where you are planted by God. He will bless you greatly and will remove you from circumstances if that is His will.

THE PRECEPT – GENEROSITY

It is not the size of the gift but the generosity of the giver. Sometimes the most generous gift is given from the heart of the giver out of enormous poverty. We read earlier about the widow who gave the two coins as Jesus watched and the woman who gave Elijah her last morsel of food.

The Apostle Paul provides another great example of generous giving from a position of poverty. 1 Corinthians 8:1 – 5:

"Moreover, brethren, we make known to you the grace of God bestowed on the churches of Macedonia. That in a great trial of affliction the abundance of their joy and their deep poverty abounded in the riches of their liberality. For I bear witness that according to their ability, yes, and beyond their ability, they were freely willing, imploring us with much urgency that we would receive the gift and the fellowship of the ministering to the saints. And not only as we had hoped, but they first gave of themselves to the Lord, and then to us by the will of God."

They gave themselves first, their hearts, and then gave joyously and generously.

THE PRECEPT – FAITHFULNESS

To be found faithful is the epitome of stewardship. Paul was faithful with the gospel through hardships, beatings, imprisonment and ultimately death. He identified other faithful servants in his letters: the Ephesians, Timothy and Epaphras, *"a faithful minister of Christ"* Colossians 1:7

Matthew quoted Jesus regarding the servants who had received the five and the two talents: *"Well done, good and faithful servant, you were faithful over a few things, I will make you ruler over many things."* Matthew 25: 21 & 23

In the parable of the unjust steward Jesus said:

"He who is faithful in what is least is faithful also in much; and he

who is unjust in what is least is unjust also in much. Therefore if you have not been faithful in the unrighteous mammon, who will commit to your trust the true riches?" Luke 16:10 & 11

Paul wrote to the Christians in Colossi *"To the saints and faithful brethren in Christ"* Colossians 1:2

Yeshua spoke to the Apostle John as recorded in Revelation 2:10:

"Do not fear ... Be faithful until death, and I will give you the crown of life."

THE PRECEPT - SERVICE

The Apostle Paul said that we are to be ambassadors for Christ:

"Now then, we are ambassadors for Christ, as though God were pleading through us; we implore you on Christ's behalf, be reconciled to God." 2 Corinthians 5:20

To serve as an ambassador means to serve with single minded service and loyalty. You simply cannot serve two masters.

"No servant can serve two masters, for either he will hate the one and love the other, or he will be loyal to the one and despise the other. You cannot serve God and mammon." Luke 16:13

What does exclusive and devoted service involve? Everything. The putting aside one's self, such as personal ambitions, comfort, dreams and desires. As Paul puts it, giving your body and mind:

"I beseech you therefore, brethren, by the mercies of God, that you present your bodies a living sacrifice, holy, acceptable to God, which

is you reasonable service. And do not be conformed to this world, but be transformed by the renewing of your mind, that you may prove what is that good and acceptable and perfect will of God." Romans 12:1-2

It is easy to get distracted from our service as ambassadors, when we get caught up in the cares of this life. God tells us to focus daily upon Him.

When I was growing up in Columbus, Georgia I attended Eastern Heights Baptist Church, from about age 8 until I left Columbus at the age of 18. Brother Altman, as we referred to him, was my first Pastor at this church. He had established a program for the Church called "Royal Ambassadors" (RA's).

This was a program whereby young men and boys came together for sports and fellowship, but most importantly for Bible study.

RA's had a great impact upon my young life, as it is where I first discovered that I could be an ambassador for Christ and that God wanted me to be His ambassador. I accepted Christ at the age of ten.

Unfortunately this program, which was present at most Southern Baptist Churches at that time, has been discontinued.

The only way that we have a chance of conforming to this precept is to abide with Christ, read and meditate on His Word, and talk with Him through constant and unceasing prayer.

"If anyone desires to come after Me, let him deny himself, and take up his cross daily and follow Me." Luke 9:23

Other precepts found in the Word:

The following is a listing of over twenty-five additional precepts regarding stewardship which I have identified in God's Word.

There are more I am sure, but these will help form a foundation and will support the principles set forth earlier. The only explanation they really need comes from the Word of God.

THE PRECEPT:

1. USE WHAT GOD HAS GIVEN

"Again, the Kingdom of Heaven can be illustrated by the story of a man going on a trip. He called together his servants and gave them money to invest for him while he was gone. He gave five bags of gold to one, two bags of gold to another, and one bag of gold to the last-dividing it in proportion to their abilities-and then left on his trip.

The servant who received the five bags of gold began immediately to invest the money and soon doubled it. The servant with two bags of gold also went right to work and doubled the money. But the servant who received the one bag of gold dug a hole in the ground and hid the master's money for safekeeping.

After a long time their master returned from his trip and called them to give an account of how they had used his money. The servant to whom he had entrusted the five bags of gold said, 'Sir, you gave me five bags of gold to invest, and I have doubled the amount.' The master was full of praise. 'Well done, my good and faithful servant. You have been faithful in handling this small amount, so now I will give you many more responsibilities. Let's celebrate together!'

Next came the servant who had received the two bags of gold, with the report, 'Sir, you gave me two bags of gold to invest, and I have doubled the amount.'

The master said, 'Well done, my good and faithful servant. You have been faithful in handling this small amount, so now I will give you many more responsibilities. Let's celebrate together!'

Then the servant with the one bag of gold came and said, 'Sir, I know you are a hard man, harvesting crops you didn't plant and gathering crops you didn't cultivate. I was afraid I would lose your money, so I hid it in the earth and here it is.'

But the master replied, 'You wicked and lazy servant! You think I'm a hard man, do you, harvesting crops I didn't plant and gathering crops I didn't cultivate?

Well, you should at least have put my money into the bank so I could have some interest. Take the money from this servant and give it to the one with the ten bags of gold

To those who use well what they are given, even more will be given, and they will have an abundance. But from those who are unfaithful, even what little they have will be taken away. Now throw this useless servant into outer darkness, where there will be weeping and gnashing of teeth.'" Matthew 25:14-30

"Unless you are faithful in small matters, you won't be faithful in large ones. If you cheat even a little, you won't be honest with greater responsibilities. And if you are untrustworthy about worldly wealth, who will trust you with the true riches of heaven? And if you are not faithful with other people's money, why should you be trusted with money of your own?" Luke 16:10-12

2. WE MUST WORK

God is a "worker". He describes Himself as a worker as well as creator in His first introduction of himself to us.

> *"So the creation of the heavens and the earth and everything in them was completed. On the seventh day, having finished his task, God rested from all his **work**. And God blessed the seventh day and declared it holy, because it was the day when he rested from his **work** of creation."* Genesis 2:1-3

I believe that the placement of God's disclosure makes it important. Jesus also described God as a worker and Himself as a co-worker. Again, this makes work important, essential and good.

> *"But Jesus replied, 'My Father never stops working, so why should I?'"* John 5:17

> *"Then Jesus explained: 'My nourishment comes from doing the will of God, who sent me, and from finishing his work.'"* John 4:34

God created man as His "co-worker":

> *"The Lord God placed the man in the Garden of Eden to tend and care for it."* Genesis 2:15

This was before Adam's original sin, the "fall" of mankind. God's assignment for man to be His "co-worker" and to perform the work of ruling God's creation in His place came at God's very creation of man. Thus man was made to be a steward for God, an assignment unique to man and I believe the first Biblical principle.

Man's work however took on a more unpleasant character as a result of the "fall".

"And to Adam he said, 'Because you listened to your wife and ate the fruit I told you not to eat, I have placed a curse on the ground. All your life you will struggle to scratch a living from it. It will grow thorns and thistles for you, though you will eat of its grains.

All your life you will sweat to produce food, until your dying day. Then you will return to the ground from which you came. For you were made from dust, and to the dust you will return.'" Genesis 3:17-19

3. WE ARE TO WORK.

"...we beg you to love them more and more. This should be your ambition: to live a quiet life, minding your own business and working with your hands, just as we commanded you before.

As a result, people who are not Christians will respect the way you live, and you will not need to depend on others to meet your financial needs." 1 Thessalonians 4:10-12

"But I replied, 'The God of heaven will help us succeed. We his servants will start rebuilding this wall. But you have no stake or claim in Jerusalem.'" Nehemiah 2:20

"And to Adam he said, 'Because you listened to your wife and ate the fruit I told you not to eat, I have placed a curse on the ground. All your life you will struggle to scratch a living from it. It will grow thorns and thistles for you, though you will eat of its grains.

All your life you will sweat to produce food, until your dying day. Then you will return to the ground from which you came. For you were made from dust, and to the dust you will return.'" Genesis 3:17-19

"Don't try to get rich by extortion or robbery. And if your wealth increases, don't make it the center of your life. God has spoken plainly, and I have heard it many times: Power, O God, belongs to you; unfailing love, O Lord, is yours. Surely you judge all people according to what they have done." Psalm 62:10-12

"Even while we were with you, we gave you this rule: 'Whoever does not work should not eat.' Yet we hear that some of you are living idle lives, refusing to work and wasting time meddling in other people's business. In the name of the Lord Jesus Christ, we appeal to such people-no, we command them: Settle down and get to work. Earn your own living." 2 Thessalonians 3:10-12

4. WORK HARD

"A lazy person is as bad as someone who destroys things." Proverbs 18:9

"I walked by the field of a lazy person, the vineyard of one lacking sense. I saw that it was overgrown with thorns. It was covered with weeds, and its walls were broken down. Then, as I looked and thought about it, I learned this lesson: A little extra sleep, a little more slumber, a little folding of the hands to rest-and poverty will pounce on you like a bandit; scarcity will attack you like an armed robber." Proverbs 24:30-34

5. PREPARE YOURSELF

"Do you see any truly competent workers? They will serve kings rather than ordinary people." Proverbs 22:29

"Work hard so God can approve you. Be a good worker, one who does not need to be ashamed and who correctly explains the word of truth." 2 Timothy 2:15

6. PLAN

"But don't begin until you count the cost. For who would begin construction of a building without first getting estimates and then checking to see if there is enough money to pay the bills? Otherwise, you might complete only the foundation before running out of funds.

And then how everyone would laugh at you! They would say, 'There's the person who started that building and ran out of money before it was finished!'" Luke 14:28-30

7. DON'T GUARANTEE OR CO-SIGN

"Do not co-sign another person's note or put up a guarantee for someone else's loan." Proverbs 22:26

"It is poor judgment to co-sign a friend's note, to become responsible for a neighbor's debts." Proverbs 17:18

"Guaranteeing a loan for a stranger is dangerous; it is better to refuse than to suffer later." Proverbs 11:15

8. DON'T FORM PARTNERSHIPS WITH UNBELIEVERS

"Don't team up with those who are unbelievers. How can goodness be a partner with wickedness? How can light live with darkness?" 2 Corinthians 6:14

9. TRAIN OTHERS

"You have heard me teach many things that have been confirmed by many reliable witnesses. Teach these great truths to trustworthy people who are able to pass them on to others." 2 Timothy 2:2

10. PAY A FAIR WAGE

"For listen! Hear the cries of the field workers whom you have cheated of their pay. The wages you held back cry out against you. The cries of the reapers have reached the ears of the Lord Almighty." James 5:4

"For the Scripture says, 'Do not keep an ox from eating as it treads out the grain.' And in another place, "Those who work deserve their pay!" 1 Timothy 5:18

11. PAY TIMELY

"Never take advantage of poor laborers, whether fellow Israelites or foreigners living in your towns. Pay them their wages each day before sunset because they are poor and are counting on it. Otherwise they might cry out to the Lord against you, and it would be counted against you as sin." Deuteronomy 24:14

12. BE CONTENT WITH YOUR WAGES

"'What should we do?' asked some soldiers. John replied, 'Don't extort money, and don't accuse people of things you know they didn't do. And be content with your pay.'" Luke 3:14

13. KEEP A SCHEDULE

"Teach us to make the most of our time, so that we may grow in wisdom." Psalms 90:12

14. BE ORDERLY

"But be sure that everything is done properly and in order." 1 Corinthians 14:40

15. TAKE TIME OFF

"Work for six days, and rest on the seventh. This will give your ox and your donkey a chance to rest. It will also allow the people of your household, including your slaves and visitors, to be refreshed." Exodus 23:12

16. PROVIDE QUALITY SERVICE

"If a soldier demands that you carry his gear for a mile, carry it two miles." Matthew 5:41

17. SEEK COUNSEL

"Without wise leadership, a nation falls; with many counselors, there is safety." Proverbs 11:14

18. DELEGATE

"'This is not good!' his father-in-law exclaimed. 'You're going to wear yourself out-and the people, too. This job is too heavy a burden for you to handle all by yourself. Now let me give you a word of advice, and may God be with you.

You should continue to be the people's representative before God, bringing him their questions to be decided. You should tell them God's decisions, teach them God's laws and instructions, and show them how to conduct their lives. But find some capable, honest men who fear God and hate bribes.

Appoint them as judges over groups of one thousand, one hundred, fifty, and ten. These men can serve the people, resolving all the ordinary cases. Anything that is too important or too complicated can be brought to you. But they can take care of the smaller matters themselves.

They will help you carry the load, making the task easier for you. If you follow this advice, and if God directs you to do so, then you will be able to endure the pressures, and all these people will go home in peace.'" Exodus 18:17-23

19. LEAD A QUIET LIFE AND ATTEND TO YOUR WORK

"Indeed, your love is already strong toward all the Christians in all of Macedonia. Even so, dear brothers and sisters, we beg you to love them more and more. This should be your ambition: to live a quiet life, minding your own business and working with your hands, just as we commanded you before. As a result, people who are not Christians will respect the way you live, and you will not need to depend on others to meet your financial needs." 1 Thessalonians 4:10-12

20. PAY YOUR BILLS

"Just as the rich rule the poor, so the borrower is servant to the lender." Proverbs 22:7 *(unpaid bills produce financial bondage) "The wicked borrow and never repay, but the godly are generous givers...."* Psalms 37:21

21. OUR BEHAVIOR SHOULD BE HOLY

As obedient children, do not be conformed to the former lusts {which were yours} in your ignorance, but like the Holy One who called you, be holy yourselves also in all {your} behavior; because it is written, "YOU SHALL BE HOLY, FOR I AM HOLY." 1 Pet 1:14-16

22. OUR BODIES SHOULD BE PURE

"Therefore I urge you, brethren, by the mercies of God, to present your bodies a living and holy sacrifice, acceptable to God, {which is} your spiritual service of worship.

And do not be conformed to this world, but be transformed by the renewing of your mind, so that you may prove what the will of God is, that which is good and acceptable and perfect." Romans 12:1-2

23. OUR MIND SHOULD NOT BE HOSTILE

"And although you were formerly alienated and hostile in mind, {engaged} in evil deeds, yet He has now reconciled you in His fleshly body through death, in order to present you before Him holy and blameless and beyond reproach" Colossians 1:21-22

24. WE SHOULD HAVE INTEGRITY

"O Lord, who may abide in your tent? Who may dwell on your holy hill?   He who walks with integrity, and works righteousness, and speaks truth in his heart. He does not slander with his tongue, nor does evil to his neighbor, nor takes up a reproach against his friend; In whose eyes a reprobate is despised, but who honors those who fear the Lord; He swears to his own hurt and does not change; He does not put out his money at interest, nor does he take a bribe against the innocent. He who does these things will never be shaken." Psalms 15:1-5

25. WE SHOULD ACKNOWLEDGE GOD

"In all your ways acknowledge Him, and He will make your paths straight." Proverbs 3:6

26. GIVE CREDIT AND THANKS TO GOD

"Whatever you do in word or deed, {do} all in the name of the Lord Jesus, giving thanks through Him to God the Father." Col 3:17

"Always giving thanks for all things in the name of our Lord Jesus Christ to God, even the Father" Ephesians 5:20

27. THINK GOOD THOUGHTS

"Finally, brethren, whatever is true, whatever is honorable, whatever is right, whatever is pure, whatever is lovely, whatever is of good repute, if there is any excellence and if anything worthy of praise, dwell on these things." Philippians 4:8

God commanded us to obey His precepts.

"He who has My commandments and keeps them is the one who loves Me; and he who loves Me will be loved by My Father, and I will love him and will disclose Myself to him." John 14:21

Through our obeying God's precepts of stewardship we again become co-workers with God. God's stewards.

Giving frees us from the familiar territory of our own needs by opening our mind to the unexplained worlds occupied by the needs of others. — Barbara Bush

STEWARDSHIP - THE PROMISES

God gave us the gift of His promises. He gave promises related to each specific Biblical principle and also promises which, although not related to a specific Biblical principle, are related to Him generally.

God also gave us the gift of the Holy Spirit, the gift of His Word, the gift of prayer, and the gift of wisdom.

God's promises and gifts became ours when we accepted Christ as our Lord and Savior. We must however know them, claim them, and act upon them. How do we do this?

1. Spend time reading God's Word to discover the promises and gifts.

2. Take each promise literally, to mean exactly what it says.

3. Confess your sins and therefore place your heart in a condition to believe the promise.

4. Claim the promise through prayer in the name of Jesus.

5. If the promise requires some action on your part – do it.

6. Believe.

7. Allow God to answer in His time.

Our life as a Christian rests upon God's promises while obeying His precepts, which flow from His principles, which mirror God's moral character, which emanates from His Person. In this way we can be in the image of God - His steward.

Here are a few of God's promises that relate to all Biblical Principles:

WE WILL BE CONFORMED TO HIS MORAL ATTRIBUTES

"For whom He foreknew, He also predestined to become conformed to the image of His Son, that He might be the first-born among many brethren." Romans 8:29

GOD WILL PROVIDE

"He who did not spare His own son, but delivered Him up for us all, how will He not also with Him freely give us all things?" Romans 8:32

"Ask, and it shall be given to you; seek and you shall find; knock, and it shall be opened to you. For every one who asks receives, and he who seeks finds, and to him who knocks it shall be opened. Or what man is there among you, when his son shall ask him for a loaf will give him a stone? Or if he shall ask for a fish, he will not give him a snake, will he? If you then, being evil, know how to give good gifts to your children, how much more shall your Father who is in heaven give what is good to those who ask Him!" Matthew 7:7-11

"Do not be anxious then, saying "What shall we eat?" or "What shall we drink?" or "With what shall we clothe ourselves?" For all these things the Gentiles eagerly seek; for your heavenly Father knows that you need all these things. But seek first His kingdom and His righteousness; and all these things shall be added to you." Matthew 6:31-33

"And Jesus answered and said to them, "Truly I say to you, if you have faith, and do not doubt, you shall not only do what was done to the fig tree, but even if you say to this mountain, 'Be taken up and cast into the sea,' it shall happen. And everything you ask in prayer, believing, you shall receive." Matthew 21:21-22

"Truly I say to you, whoever says to this mountain, 'Be taken up and cast into the sea,' and does not doubt in his heart, but believes that what he says is going to happen, it shall be granted him. Therefore I say to you, all things for which you pray and ask, believe that you have received them, and they shall be granted you." Mark 11:23-24

PROMISIES THAT RELATE TO STEWARDSHIP:

"Therefore, obey the terms of this covenant so that you will prosper in everything you do." Deuteronomy 29:9

"Whoever gives to the poor will lack nothing. But a curse will come upon those who close their eyes to poverty." Proverbs 28:27

"Feed the hungry and help those in trouble. Then your light will shine out from the darkness, and the darkness around you will be as bright as day. The Lord will guide you continually, watering your life when you are dry and keeping you healthy, too. You will be like a well-watered garden, like an ever-flowing spring." Isaiah 58:10-11

"If you give, you will receive. Your gift will return to you in full measure, pressed down, shaken together to make room for more, and running over. Whatever measure you use in giving--large or small-- it will be used to measure what is given back to you." Luke 6:38

"And this same God who takes care of me will supply all your needs from his glorious riches, which have been given to us in Christ Jesus." Philippians 4:19

"And so I tell you, keep on asking, and you will be given what you ask for. Keep on looking, and you will find. Keep on knocking, and the door will be opened." Luke 11:9

"Sell what you have and give to those in need. This will store up treasure for you in heaven! And the purses of heaven have no holes in them. Your treasure will be safe-no thief can steal it and no moth can destroy it." Luke 12:33

"You can ask for anything in my name, and I will do it, because the work of the Son brings glory to the Father. Yes, ask anything in my name, and I will do it!" John 14:13-14

"At that time you won't need to ask me for anything. The truth is, you can go directly to the Father and ask him, and he will grant your request because you use my name. You haven't done this before. Ask, using my name, and you will receive, and you will have abundant joy." John 16:23-24

If we continuously focus on God's promises as we abide with Him in prayer, everything about us will change. We will stop praying and asking for material things and begin to ask God to do His will in and through us for His honor and for His glory.

GOD GAVE US THE GIFT OF PRAYER

Many books have been written and numerous sermons delivered by great people of God on the subject of prayer. It is probably the most written about subject in Christian literature. I encourage you to seek some of these books out and read them.

I cannot add to what these writers have written about prayer, this very important gift from God, but I can quote from one man of God whose life demonstrated that he knew about prayer.

Oswald Chambers died at the young age of forty-three in the foreign land of Egypt, while with the Y.M.C.A. as chaplain to British soldiers during World War One.

He died of complications following an emergency appendectomy. He was never famous during his life-time. All of his well-known books, including _My Upmost for His Highest,_ were published after his death, through transcriptions of his lectures and sermons by his wife, Gertrude "Biddy" Hobbs.

Oswald devoted his life in service to Jesus Christ.

What follows is a message from Oswald Chambers as copied from his book _If you will Ask ... Reflections on the Power of Prayer,_ given to troops, November 1915, YMCA Camp Zeitoun, Egypt.

> _"Only when a man flounders beyond any grip of himself and cannot understand things does he really pray. Prayer is not part of the natural life. By "natural" I mean the ordinary, sensible, healthy, worldly, minded life._
>
> _Some say that a man will suffer in his life if he does not pray. I question it. Prayer is an interruption of personal ambition, and no person who is busy has time to pray. What will suffer is the life of God in him, which is nourished not by food but by prayer._
>
> _If we look on prayer as a means of developing ourselves, there is nothing in it at all, and we do not find that idea in the Bible. Prayer is other than meditation; it develops the life of God in us. When a man is born from above, the life of the Son of God begins in him, and he can either starve that life or nourish it._
>
> _It is not so true that "Prayer changes things" as that prayer changes me, and then I change things; consequently we must not ask God to do what He has created us to do._
>
> _For instance, Jesus Christ is not a social reformer, He came to alter us first, and if there is any social reform to be done on earth, we must do it._

God has so constituted things that prayer on the basis of redemption alters the way a man looks at things. Prayer is not a question of altering things externally, but of working wonders in a man's disposition. When you pray, things remain the same, but you begin to be different.

The good of praying is that it gets us to know God and enables God to perform His order through us, no matter what His permissive will may be. A man is never what he is in spite of his circumstances, but because of them. Circumstances are like feather beds – very comfortable to be on top of, but immensely smothering if they get on top of you. Jesus Christ, by the Spirit of God, always keeps us on top of our circumstances.

What's the Good of Prayer?

We need it-Luke 11:1.
    Human wits have an end-Psalm 107:13, 19, 28.
    Human wills have an end-Romans 8:26.
    Human wisdom has an end-James 1:5.

        Prayer alters me.

We must do it-Luke 18:1.
    If we would know God-Matthew 6:8.
    If we would help men-John 14:12-13.
    If we would do God's will-1 John 5:14-16.

        Prayer alters others.

We can do it-James 5:16.
    By asking-John 15:7.
    By seeking-Luke 11:9-13.
    By knocking.

        Prayer alters circumstances through me."[x]

Jack R. Taylor made, what he called "four points of perspective", in the introduction to his book on prayer entitled *Prayer: Life's Limitless Reach*:

> "1. No believer's spiritual life will rise to stay above the level of his praying.
>
> 2. No church's ultimate effectiveness will rise to stay above the level of its corporate prayer life.
>
> 3. No church's corporate prayer life will be greater than the personal prayer lives of those who make up its constituency.
>
> 4. No believer's prayer life will rise to stay above the level of his or her own personal, regular, daily time of worship with God."[xi]

Pointed perspectives on prayer for every believer and for every church.

GOD GAVE US THE GIFT OF HIS WORD

The Bible, written over a time period of approximately 1400 years, in various geographical locations from Italy in the west to perhaps Persia in the east, by writers, not only from the various times and cultures, but of such diverse backgrounds as kings, prophets, statesmen, herdsmen, fishermen, physician, and others, is a supernatural book of divine origin in which God reveals Himself to man.

As Norman Geisler states in his book *Christian Apologetics*, the Bible is inspired, meaning God-breathed (II Tim 3:16) and Spirit-moved (II Peter 1:20-21):

"Inspiration Is Verbal.

It was not merely the thoughts or the oral pronouncements of the prophets that were inspired but the very "words." Moses "wrote all the words of the Lord" (Exod. 24:4) and David confessed, "His word is upon my tongue" (11 Sam. 23:2). Jeremiah was told to ".diminish not a word" (Jer. 26:2 KJV). Jesus repeated over and over that the authority was found in what "is written" (see Matt. 4:4, 7). Paul testified that he spoke in "words ... taught by the Spirit" (I Cor. 2:13). And the classic text in II Timothy 3:16 declares that it is the "writings," the graphe, that are inspired of God.

Inspiration Is Plenary.

Jesus not only affirmed the written revelation of God but he taught that the whole (complete, entire) Old Testament was inspired of God. Everything including Moses and the prophets is from God (Matt. 5:17, 18) and must be fulfilled (Luke 24:44). Paul added that "whatever was written in former days [in the Old Testament] was written for our instruction" (Rom. 15:4) and that "all scripture is inspired of God" and therefore "profitable for teaching, for reproof, for correction, and for training in righteousness" (11 Tim. 3:16, 17).

That is to say, the inspiration of the Bible extends to everything it teaches whether spiritual or factual. Of course, not everything contained in the Bible is taught by the Bible. The Bible contains a true record of Satan's lies (see Gen. 3:4), but the Bible is not thereby teaching that these lies are true. Plenary inspiration means only that whatever the Bible teaches is true, is actually true.

Inspiration Conveys Authority.

Further, the authority of the Bible's teaching flows from its divine origin as the oracles or Word of God (see Rom. 3:2). Jesus said of the Old Testament, *"The scriptures cannot be broken"* for they are the *"word of God"* (John 10:35). Jesus claimed the authority of *"it is written"* for his teaching over and over again (cf. Matt. 22:29; Mark 9:12). He resisted the devil by the same written authority (see Matt. 4:4, 7, 10).

The written Word, then, is the authority of God for settling all disputes of doctrine or practice. It is God's Word in man's words; it is divine truth in human terms.

Inspiration Implies the Inerrancy of the Teaching.

Jesus believed that God's Word is true (John 17:17) and the apostles taught that God cannot lie (Heb. 6:18). Furthermore, Jesus affirmed that every "iota and dot" of the Old Testament was from God. Simply put: whatever God utters is true and without error.

The original writings of the Old Testament are the utterance of God through men. Therefore, the writings of the Old Testament are the inerrant Word of God. This is what both Jesus and the apostles taught with divine authority, an authority confirmed by the unique concurrence of three miracles in the life, death, and resurrection of Christ."[xii]

God gave us the gift of His word. Read it.

GOD GIVES US THE GIFT OF WISDOM

I now live in South Georgia, and the nearest airport is in Tallahassee, Florida, about a 45 minute drive from my house. The problem is that the Tallahassee airport has limited service. No international flights and domestic flights to just a few airports.

Of the 800 thousand passengers who annually fly out of this airport about 200 thousand of these passengers fly into the Hartsfield-Jackson Atlanta International Airport. Why? Because you can fly most anywhere from the Atlanta airport. In fact over 100 million passengers each year fly out of this airport making it the busiest airport in the world. It has held this distinction since 1998.

So generally when I am flying I drive to Atlanta, about a four hour drive, and catch a flight. It is easier, cheaper, and most times quicker, than driving 45 minutes to Tallahassee, waiting over two hours for a flight (if it is not delayed or canceled) and flying to Atlanta for a connecting flight.

When I am waiting for my Atlanta flight to board I often stare out the window at all of the aircraft traffic. It is amazing to see all the activity and how it all seems to flow seamlessly, so that each aircraft lands, takes off and makes it to and from its assigned gate without a hitch.

One cannot make heads or tails of this massive operation by simply watching from a terminal window. But, if you are privileged to go up to the airport control tower, the highest airport tower in the USA at almost 400 feet tall, you will see all of the 192 gates, five parallel runways, parking and other amenities sitting on 4700 acres. If the weather is clear you can even see downtown Atlanta which sits about seven miles to the northeast.

What you also will see there are blinking blips of lights on the radar screen representing all of the aircraft in the area for about a one hundred mile radius, and a screen showing all of the aircraft on the ground. You can also observe as the airport controllers direct each and every movement of each and every aircraft on the screen.

That is how air traffic flows so seamlessly, without a hitch. The reason for every aircraft movement then becomes apparent once you see and grasp the overall picture.

A mistake that some Christians make is to believe that this is an illustration of what God provides us when He gives the gift of wisdom. That is, to think that God's gift of wisdom provides an insight into the meaning and purpose of the events of life, and to believe that one can know why God does what He does in each particular event. In other words, to be in God's control tower.

I'm sorry to report that this is not what is meant by the gift of wisdom from God. According to J.I. Packer in his book _Knowing God_ wisdom is more like learning to drive.

"What matters in driving is the speed and appropriateness of your reactions to things and the soundness of your judgment as to what scope a situation gives you. You do not ask yourself why the road should narrow or screw itself into a clog leg wiggle just where it does, nor why that van should be parked where it is, nor why the driver in front should hug the crown of the road so lovingly; you simply try to see and do the right thing in the actual situation that presents itself. The effect of divine wisdom is to enable you and me to do just that in the actual situations of everyday life." [xiii]

To expand on Packer's illustration: The longer we drive the better we are at making the appropriate decision at the moment it is needed.

Packer goes on to explain what he believes wisdom is.

"God's work of giving wisdom is a means to his chosen end of restoring and perfecting the relationship between himself and human beings - the relationship for which he made them. For what is this wisdom that he gives?

As we have seen, it is not a sharing in all his knowledge, but a disposition to confess that he is wise, and to cleave to him and live for him in the light of his Word through thick and thin.

Thus the effect of his gift of wisdom is to make us more humble, more joyful, more godly, more quick-sighted as to his will, more resolute in the doing of it and less troubled (not less sensitive, but less bewildered) than we were at the dark and painful things of which our life in this fallen world is full.

The New Testament tells us that the fruit of wisdom is Christlikeness, peace, humility, and love. The root of it is faith in Christ (I Cor. 3:18; 2 Tim 3:15) as the manifested wisdom of God (1 Cor. 1:24, 30).

Thus, the kind of wisdom that God waits to give to those who ask him is a wisdom that will bind us to himself, a wisdom that will find expression in a spirit of faith and a life of faithfulness."[xiv]

Wisdom therefore, is accepting:

- that God is God;

- that we will never understand His ways;

"Oh, the depth of the riches both of the wisdom and knowledge of God! How unsearchable are His judgments and unfathomable His ways! For WHO HAS KNOWN THE MIND OF THE LORD, OR WHO BECAME HIS COUNSELOR?" Romans 11:33-34

- that life is difficult, and; that we are to trust in God and walk daily in His fellowship.

"Trust in the LORD with all your heart and do not lean on your own understanding. In all your ways acknowledge Him, and He will make your paths straight. Do not be wise in your own eyes; fear the LORD

and turn away from evil. It will be healing to your body and refreshment to your bones." Proverbs 3:5-8

THE GIFT OF THE HOLY SPIRIT

I am writing here about the gift **of** the Holy Spirit and not the gifts **from** the Holy Spirit. Acts 2:38 states:

"Then Peter said to them, "Repent, and let every one of you be baptized in the name of Jesus Christ for the remission of sins, and you shall receive the gift of the Holy Spirit."

Jesus promised us the Holy Spirit in John 14:16 & 18:

"And I will pray the Father, and He will give you another Helper that He may abide with you forever - I will not leave you orphans; I will come to you."

Two questions come to mind: (1) how do we receive the gift of the Holy Spirit? And (2) what does it mean to receive the gift of the Holy Spirit?

God answered these two questions through the Apostle Paul. When a person accepts Jesus Christ as his Lord and savior they are baptized with the Holy Spirit as written in Acts 2:38 quoted above and also by Paul in these verses:

1 Corinthians 12:13: *"For by one Spirit we were all baptized into one body ... "* Romans 8:9: *"But you are not in the flesh but in the Spirit, if indeed the Spirit of God dwells in you. Now if anyone does not have the Spirit of Christ, he is not His."*

Therefore at the moment of salvation we receive the Holy Spirit. There is no separate baptism of the Holy Spirit apart from salvation.

When the apostle Paul wrote further about the Holy Spirit he commanded believers to "be filled with the Spirit". What exactly did he mean by "filled"?

He was writing about being constantly filled.

If a vessel is filled, how can it be constantly being filled?

Someone gave this example to me, I think it must have been my former pastor Dr. Bob Kleinschmidt:

If you fill a vessel with rocks and then pour in water until it is full, one could say that it was filled with water. However if you start to remove the rocks you can continually fill the vessel with more and more water so that it remains filled with water. This is a constant filling.

So if we are filled with the Spirit but we are constantly confessing our sins, removing the rocks, we can be continually being filled with the Spirit. I think this is what Paul had in mind.

God gave us the gift of the Holy Spirit at our salvation, therefore continue to be constantly filled by the confession of sin. To be filled is to live in the very presence of Yeshua. Sin and God cannot occupy the same space.

What does it mean to have the Holy Spirit? It means to have God in us and to live Christ-likeness.

My take on tithing in America is that it's a middle-class way of robbing God. Tithing to the church and spending the rest on your family is not a Christian goal. It's a diversion. The real issue is: How shall we use God's trust fund — namely, all we have — for His glory? In a world with so much misery, what lifestyle should we call our people to live? What example are we setting? — John Piper

GENEROUS

Before discussing becoming a generous giver, a word or two about debt. What is it? **Money owed to anyone for anything**. It can be categorized as: 1. Consumer debt (unpaid utility bills, credit card bills, gambling debt, car loans ... debt from anything we have consumed); 2. Real estate or mortgage debt for our home; or 3. Investment debt, including business debt. Is debt a sin? God does not prohibit debt in His Word. He does not encourage it either. He does seem to discourage its use.

The problem is not debt, which is usually only a symptom of the actual problem(s). The issue is what motivated us to incur the debt. Some possibilities include greed, self-indulgence, lack of patience, etc. These motivations are prohibited by God.

Any debt always encumbers the future and the danger of compounding interest could lead to financial ruin. Business or investment debt, which produces a rate of return greater than the cost of borrowing, can justify incurring the debt. Many times home ownership via a mortgage will financially justify the debt. Most consumer debt, if not all, cannot be financially justified, and is the most likely to be wrongfully motivated. Since consumer debt usually produces no financial return it is also the most likely form of debt to lead to financial ruin for the borrower.

What do I mean by "the danger of compounding interest?" This is the banker's key to financial success and the borrower's slippery slope to financial ruin.

When somebody once asked Albert Einstein if nuclear power was the greatest power in the world, he answered, "there is no greater power known to man than compounding interest."

Let's say you borrow $20,000 to buy a car and agree to pay it back over five years at 12.5% interest. Your monthly payment will be about $450 and you will actually repay the bank $27,000 over the five years ($450 x 60). This $7,000 in interest payment sounds like a lot but that's not the end of the story. The bank will take your $450 each month and loan it out again at 12.5% interest and at the end of the five years will have accumulated $75,000. Compound interest, interest on interest, makes the bank a nice profit. Your cost for the debt therefore is not the $7,000 you paid the bank in interest, but $55,000. I say this because if you had started saving the $450 per month instead of buying the car on credit you would have earned the 12.5% interest. Compound interest would have worked in your favor. At the end of the five years you would have the $75,000 and not the bank. At this point you could pay cash for the car and have $55,000 left in your savings account ... still earning more interest.

Credit card debt is even more dramatic as you generally will pay an interest rate greater than 12.5%. Debt leads to financial bondage while saving leads to financial freedom. Avoid debt whenever possible. A little sacrifice by delaying purchases and saving the money instead will, over time, pay great rewards.

Compounding interest is the secret. Here's a living example as written by Dr. Paul B. Farrell in a CBS Market Watch article dated July 27, 1999.

"When we were born, my grandparents put $1,000 in a mutual fund for my sisters and then for me. After all, back in 1938 ... $1,000 was a lot of money! It represented half a year's income for most people. My grandparents were not well-off. Comfortable yes, well-off no. What they did for each of us was a definite sacrifice on their part. Now I'm 60 years old and haven't touched it yet. How's it doing? Well, not bad. Not bad at all. Last statement showed just a bit over $1.8 million (all taxes have been paid from dividends, etc.) My older sister's money was put into a less conservative fund, and when she turned 65 she finally decided to "tap" it. She had a touch under $5 million."

GIVE

Saving, instead of consuming via debt, also leads to opportunities to give.

> *"The wicked borrow and never repay, but the godly are generous givers."* Psalm 37:21

> *"Honor the LORD with your wealth and with the best part of everything your land produces. Then he will fill your barns with grain, and your vats will overflow with the finest wine."* Prov. 3:9-10

> *"The generous prosper and are satisfied; those who refresh others will themselves be refreshed."* Proverbs 11:25

> *"Those who shut their ears to the cries of the poor will be ignored in their own time of need."* Proverbs 21:13

> *"You must each make up your own mind as to how much you should give. Don't give reluctantly or in response to pressure. For God loves the person who gives cheerfully."* 2 Corinthians 9:7

> *"Then the King will say to those on the right, 'Come, you who are blessed by my Father, inherit the Kingdom prepared for you from the foundation of the world. For I was hungry, and you fed me. I was thirsty, and you gave me a drink. I was a stranger, and you invited me into your home. I was naked, and you gave me clothing. I was sick, and you cared for me. I was in prison, and you visited me.'"* Matthew 25:34-36

If you really believe that God owns everything and that we as His stewards have the responsibility of administrating God's property, giving takes on new meaning.

False teaching is always destructive to the Church. Jesus was passionate when warning people about false teaching and spoke of serious consequences to those that would lead others astray. Money always carries with it the potential for greed, manipulation and self-interest.

There are two areas of concern about teaching on giving in the Church today that have detrimental consequences to the Church, believers, and the perception of Christianity in society. These two areas peg opposite ends of a continuum I'll call "teaching on giving."

On one end of the continuum I place "The Prosperity Gospel" and on the other end, I'll call it "The Legalistic Tithe." Both of these messages contain false biblical concepts. Both have kernels of truth, biblical themes and familiar terms but the doctrine is profoundly false.

"The Prosperity Gospel" teaches in essence that "I can control God." It is a self-centered approach to giving where the end goal is really to get something back for oneself. Giving does not emanate from a heart filled with love for God and others, but instead is filled with love for oneself.

The motivations are compromised on both sides where the leaders' goals are to manipulate people into giving more money by appealing to their self-interest and desire for receiving prosperity in return for giving to God.

Note that in "The Prosperity Gospel", believing that God loves to prosper His children, reward their generosity and pours out His blessing upon those who are generous and share with others is not wrong. But giving motivated, not by love for God or others, but rather for one's own benefit clearly misses the heart of giving and the meaning of stewardship in God's Word.

So many watchers, listeners, and readers have been sucked in by this false doctrine and have given so much money to the scam artists who preach this "theology", that it is tempting to write at length about how false it is.

However, I think that it is so obviously false that if any Christian thinks about it for a moment, they would change channels, switch to another radio station or buy a different book.

However, God did say that the day would come when people would have "itching ears". (2 Timothy 4:3&4). That they would seek after teachers whose message feeds their narcissistic desires. That day is obviously today.

Because of this and other events, I believe that we can expect the soon return of Jesus. But, that is the topic for another book.

"The Legalistic Tithe" teaches a legalistic approach to giving whereby people are taught a formula for "right giving": ten percent belongs to God and goes to the local church. Some people feel guilt and judgment if they are not giving up to the tithe and others who give at the tithe level have a false sense that giving ten percent, regardless of heart condition, fulfills their obligation to God. Often there is a belief they are paid up in full and the rest of the 90% is theirs to do with as they please.

It is important to note that tithing as a part of a giving discipline is not wrong in itself, in fact it can be a very useful and practical part of a believers giving convictions. The problem arises when it is taught as a commandment and as the beginning and end of God's acceptable standard today.

Teaching such a doctrine is simply inaccurate.

Sadly, when people buy into an over-simplified formulaic style of legalistic tithing, they fall into the same trap as the Pharisees. They miss the glorious reality of freedom in Christ that Jesus ushered in as the New Covenant as well as all the wonderful values Jesus and the Apostles taught that brought an abundance of love and mercy into the practice of giving.

Some Pastor/teachers even mix the two false doctrines. Claiming first that tithing is required by God, therefore putting guilt and pressure on the listener to give ten percent and avoid God's punishment, while also claiming that if they do tithe, they will reap financial rewards. Thus, appealing to the greed of the listener. Some preachers even put up videos of testimonies from people who were once financial failures, but then began tithing and became successful.

The old stick and carrot pitch, meant to extract as much money as possible from their audience.

By teaching these concepts the Pastor/teacher totally misses the Biblical message of following the leading of the Holy Spirit and of grace giving from the heart.

One other important point. God does not punish believers through financial failure for not following the law of tithing, or any other law. The good news of the gospel is that Jesus paid the price for our sin, any sin and all sin.

Yes, some sins have consequences in and of themselves, but if we, as born again believers, are still subject to our paying the price for sin then Christ died in vain. It may be a sin of the heart to not give, but it is not a sin, punished by failure, to not tithe.

"There is therefore now no condemnation to them which are in Christ Jesus, who walk not after the flesh, but after the Spirit" Romans 8:1

We must teach accurately, with careful discipline not to compromise God's Word. Some compromise by failing to teach about money out of fear or feelings of inadequacies. Others compromise by teaching scripture inaccurately, out of context, or sound biting passages that mislead the author's intent or alone are in conflict with the whole counsel of Scripture.

Pastor/Teachers need to be on guard against the temptations that come in teaching about money and possessions. Many, when teaching about money, are influenced by pressures (such as meeting budget), and are tempted to adjust the message for what may seem most expedient for results.

Some of the traps include teaching inaccurate legalistic standards of giving, creating feelings of pressure or obligation or even creating guilt. All of these are clearly contrary to Scripture and all of these may be tempting at one time or another to motivate people's responses.

Besides, human nature is such that when a person is freed to give what they desire rather than what is required, they give more abundantly.

As an example:

When I was working with a ministry that would annually promote its leader's book for sale, it began by offering the book, pre-publication for a required $25 donation. The exact same price that it would be selling for in the market-place when it later came to market. The ministry pre-sold 100,000 books, and received exactly $2,500,000. In a subsequent year the ministry began to offer the books pre-publication for a donation of any amount. That meant that people could donate as little as one cent and receive the book. Again, 100,000 books were pre-sold, however the ministry received over $3,500,000 of donations. Free the heart and you free the purse.

Give people rules to follow in their giving, and they will give no more than the rules require. Free the hearts of people and they respond abundantly and beyond expectations. Giving joyfully comes from the right motivation.

The concept of the tithe is no longer applicable. It was part of the Mosaic Law, and as such was a teaching tool much like the animal sacrifices. The law was done away with (John 1:16-17; Romans 6:14 and 7:1-6; II Corinthians 3:1-8; Galatians 3:19:25 and 5:18 etc.).

This is a difficult statement for many to accept; therefore, I must explain why I came to believe that the mandated tithe is not applicable to believers today and that teaching this legalistic tithe is teaching false doctrine.

Most, if not all Christian protestant churches would define the Biblical tithe to mean ten percent of gross income given to the local church to pay the workers and support the work of God through the local church.

They believe this is an unchanging biblical standard reflecting an eternal principle established by God prior to the Mosaic Law and is expected from all believers regardless of economic class.

This might be best illustrated by the position articulated by the Southern Baptist Convention. One text used by Southern Baptists to teach giving is a book by Dr. Bobby Eklund and Terry Austin entitled _Partners with God, Bible Truths about Giving._

In this book the two writers introduce the subject of tithing with a supposedly true story of a mother who murdered her two children and committed suicide when she mistakenly thought that she had terminal cancer and would soon die. Eklund & Austin write about this incident:

"Thirty-five-year-old Linda Welch stood by her mother's side and watched her suffer an excruciating death from cancer. Linda grieved as her mother's body slowly succumbed to the destructive effects of rampant diseased cells. She spent many hours trying to comfort her mother while covering up her own fear and sorrow.

Several months later, Linda developed a painful throat ailment. She believed it was cancer and was convinced that she and her children would be better off in heaven. With the feeling that she could not endure another bout with cancer, Linda reacted out of fear. She shot her children, five-year-old Crystal and ten-year-old Steven, Jr. Turning the gun to herself, she ended her own life.

The terrible irony is that an autopsy revealed Linda did not have cancer but rather strep throat and the flu. Three lives were prematurely destroyed because of a false belief.

This tragic and extreme story illustrates an important truth, believing a lie always leads to sorrow and destruction. Satan is identified as the father of all lies because deceit is one of his most effective weapons.

In the area of money management, Satan has successfully robbed many Christians of blessings by convincing them to believe a lie.

The lie simply states that tithing is an Old Testament practice which is no longer valid for the New Testament Christian. This deceit has confined many Christians to financial bondage and plundered a sizable portion of monetary resources from the church."[xv]

Wow! If this is what Southern Baptist Pastors are given to read and believe about giving, is it any wonder that they hold tenaciously to teaching their congregations the same thing?

Recently, a young Southern Baptist Pastor in the South delivered a sermon about tithing, and how it was a requirement for all believers. After sitting through this message I sent him an email. In it I shared much of what is in this book about stewardship and giving.

Some weeks later we had coffee together and he brought up the subjects of giving, my email and his message. He said that in the future, if I were to be in his church when he spoke about tithing, I should just put my hands over my ears, because he was not changing his message that tithing was required giving.

He said in so many words, "The tithe is a bedrock of Southern Baptist tradition, and I am not about to buck the system." He did not even want to discuss what the Bible had to say. He had his position and he was sticking with it. It had been taught to him for all of his time in ministry, beginning with seminary.

I did have occasion to sit under the teaching of this young pastor again when he spoke on giving. I was pleased that he gave a message very similar to any message I would have delivered. Except for about twenty seconds of the message, when he stated that the tithe was required giving by every Christian to the local church. Maybe next time, he will even lose those twenty seconds.

We really need to examine closely, and carefully understand what the Word of God actually says about the tithe, Old Testament giving, and giving after Jesus Christ.

Before discussing a subject, it is important to agree on terminology. I'm sure that we would all readily agree that the word tithe means simply "a tenth". This is also the simple definition in the Hebrew and Greek languages. Defining the Biblical definition of the tithe is less simple.

The more precise Biblical definition is different and is given in the Mosaic Law. The tithe was given from or "out of" the land production from the land given by God to the nation of Israel. It came solely from the crops of this land or from the increase of animals herded on this land – NO OTHER SOURCE. Other land was defiled and a tithe could not come from it.

The word "tithe" is used thirteen times in the Bible, and the word "tithes" appears an additional twenty-one times. Not once do you see the word "money" associated with it. There is no evidence that those who made their living from sources other than the land, such as craftsmen or sellers of merchandise, gave a tithe.

The tithe was paid by only eleven of the twelve tribes of Israel – NO OTHER PEOPLE.

Why? No other nation belonged to God nor worshiped Him. The tribe of Levi did not receive an inheritance of land in Israel. Instead the tribe of Levi was to care for the temple and to serve God as a temporary intercessory priesthood between God and the nation of Israel. The tithe was given to the tribe of Levi – they in turn gave a 10th.

The challenge to this last definition is that Abraham tithed prior to the receipt of the Mosaic Law from God (Genesis 14).

Dr. Eklund writes, *"The idea of bringing a tithe to God can be found in the very first book of the Bible (see Genesis 14:20; 28:22). It was practiced by Abraham four hundred years before Moses.*

Bringing a tenth to their god was a common exercise in many ancient societies. Man has always used the number ten as a basis for enumerating. The actual number ten represents completeness. Therefore the tithe symbolized giving our all to God."[xvi]

Any serious discussion of the Biblical tithe therefore must deal first with the pre Mosaic Law events before subsequently discussing the Mosaic Law and the New Testament or New Covenant teaching on the tithe.

I. GIVING BEFORE MOSAIC LAW

Cain and Abel – the first recorded offering.

We are not told what percentage of their harvest they offered as a gift to the Lord. In *Genesis 4:3-5*, the term "offering" is used; suggesting a voluntary or freewill gift. Cain offered some of his crops to the Lord, Abel gave the best and first of his livestock - firstborn, fattest, choice, best. Upon receiving their gifts, God knowing their hearts, accepted Abel and his gift but rejected Cain and his gift.

Abraham and Melchizadek – Genesis 14

Sometime around 2000 B.C. four kings from city-states in the area between the Tigris and Euphrates Rivers, led by Kedorlaomer king of Elam, defeated five kings from city-states within a few miles of each other at the southern end of the Dead Sea (vv. 1-3).

After twelve years of paying tribute, these five kings revolted. The next year, Kedorlaomer again led the city-kings into battle and conquered the whole region. That's when the king of Sodom together with four other kings went to battle with Kedorlaomer and the other three kings.

Kedorlaomer was again victorious. He captured Lot, Abram's nephew, with all his possessions and all the possessions of Sodom and Gomorrah.

Abram lived at the Oaks of Mamre about midway between Salem and Sodom. Upon hearing that his nephew had been taken prisoner, he took all of his servants (there were 318 trained servants) and defeated the enemy, rescued Lot and his possessions and all of the possessions that had been captured from Sodom and Gomorrah (vv. 15 - 16).

Upon returning from the battle Abram was greeted near Salem (Jerusalem) by the king of Sodom and the king of Salem, Melchizedek. Melchizedek brought bread and wine for Abram and his men and he blessed Abram (vv. 17 – 20).

Abram gave Melchizedek a tenth of all the recovered plunder and he gave the king of Sodom the remaining plunder after the men who had fought with Abram had received their share. He kept nothing for himself (vv. 21 – 24), so that the King of Sodom could never claim he was the one who made Abram rich.

Since this incident is only one of two occurrences of the tithe apart from the Mosaic Law in the Bible we should try to understand its significance and relevance

Some questions: Who was Melchizedek? Why did Abram give him 10% and give the king of Sodom 90%. What was the source of the gift? What relevance is this act over 4000 years ago to believers today?

Who was Melchizedek?

The answer to this question is shrouded in controversy. We must draw a distinction between the "historical" Melchizedek and the "typical" Melchizedek.

"Historically", Melchizedek was the king of Salem (considered by most historians to be Jerusalem) about 2000 B. C. Records do not identify his father, mother or any genealogy.

In the ancient world, this could mean that the parents were of no importance. To a Jew, one who had gentile parents was considered to be without father and without mother. Some say that Melchizedek was one of many self-appointed pagan priest-kings in his era; others conclude that he was Shem, the son of Noah, who was king and priest to those descended from him.

We just don't know.

"Typically", Melchizedek has been defined as a type of Jesus Christ as described in Psalm 110 and Hebrews 7. Some have taught that he was actually Christ in a pre-incarnate form – this view is not widely held and is refuted by most Bible commentators.

> "There is no record of his father or mother or any of his ancestors - no beginning or end to his life. He remains a priest forever, resembling the Son of God." Hebrews 7:3

We have discussed the genealogy; therefore let's turn to "no beginning or end to his life".

This should be understood "typically" because Melchizedek was not God living in the flesh before the birth of Jesus Christ. The following phrase: "resembling the Son of God", would indicate that he was not THE Son of God but a type of Christ. Jesus Christ was the Person, the event and the time when God took on flesh and lived among His creation.

Melchizedek was greater than Abram since Abram paid a tithe to Melchizedek. Ancient war custom dictated that a tenth of the spoils of war be given to the local ruler.

So did Abram follow this tradition or did he freely tithe to Melchizedek to proclaim him as a priest of his God – Yahweh?

It is unclear, but many conservative evangelical scholars such as Lewis Sperry Chafer, Charles Ryrie, Merrill Unger, and John Walvoord contend that Melchizedek was never used to validate tithing under the Mosaic Law and therefore cannot be used to validate such action under the New Covenant following Calvary.

It is quite interesting to note that Abram did not give a tithe to Melchizadek to be blessed by Melchizadek. If you read the text closely you will note that it was after he was blessed that Abram presented his gift. Likewise we do not give to God to be blessed by God. We are already blessed beyond measure by God through His son, Jesus Christ. Therefore we give with a grateful heart.

Why did Abram give Melchizedek 10% and the king of Sodom 90%? Three verses of Genesis 14 talk about Melchizedek but four verses mention the king of Sodom. The last three verses of this narrative are spoken by Abram to the king of Sodom but not one word is recorded as having been spoken by Abram to Melchizedek.

The focus is clearly on Abram's declaration to the king of Sodom. God later described Sodom in Genesis 18 *"The cry of Sodom and Gomorrah is great and **their sin is very grievous"**.

Certainly no one, not even Dr. Eklund, would suggest that this example means that after we give 10% to God we are free to give 90% to Satan, or to sinful endeavors!

Since the source of the gift was from the spoils of war, not from any earnings or other possessions of Abram, it is better to conclude that the gift was following ancient tradition regarding the division of spoils after battle. It has no connection to the Mosaic Law tithe nor to Christians today. Also Abram lived 175 years and it is nowhere written that he ever gave another gift.

This narrative regarding the tithe given by Abram and the one to follow regarding Jacob's tithe are descriptive in nature and not prescriptive. They are merely describing the events that took place and are not prescribing what anyone should do in the future.

Genesis 28

> *"Then Jacob made this vow: 'If God will be with me and protect me on this journey and give me food and clothing, and if he will bring me back safely to my father, then I will make the Lord my God.*
>
> *This memorial pillar will become a place for worshiping God, and I will give God a tenth of everything he gives me.'"*
> Genesis 28:20-22

This is certainly not a tithe from the spoils of war as in Genesis 14. Jacob clearly vowed to give a tenth of all that God gives to him. The vow was conditional and God did not ask for it as far as we know. This was a vow personal to Jacob.

Although God greatly blessed Jacob we are given no other indication that Jacob kept this vow. To whom would Jacob have given his tithe? Jacob served as his own priest as head of his household. Perhaps, if he gave a tithe, he gave to the poor.

Jacob's tithe, like Abram's tithe to Melchizedek, has no relevance to Christians today. It was a personal vow relevant only to Jacob much like many vows made today.

"Lord, save me from this situation, or do this or that and I will do such and such" - clearly important to the one making the vow, but having no relevance to others. Like the fallen hiker named Bill, in the story written earlier.

This was actually a low point spiritually for Jacob as he was trying to bribe God. He was actually attempting to buy God's blessing. Not an action that we want to emulate, but it is what "prosperity gospel" preachers say we are to do.

Now the reasoning goes, by those who claim that the tithe given by Abram and by Jacob support the requirement to tithe today, is as follows; that since giving a tithe existed before the Mosaic Law and under the Law, it therefore should exist after the Mosaic Law, because it is a transcendent, universal standard for giving ordained by God.

One obvious weakness in this thinking is that the observance of the Sabbath existed before the Law, and it existed during the time of the Mosaic Law, it was actually one of the Ten Commandments, however Christians do not observe the Sabbath after the Law.

Why? Because the New Covenant abrogates the Sabbath. To paraphrase Colossians 2: "Don't let anybody hold you to a Sabbath." And Romans 14: "One man regards the Sabbath and one doesn't, it doesn't matter."

There were animal sacrifices prior to the Law; as far back as Abel after the Garden of Eden. There were animal sacrifices during the time of the Law, however the animal sacrificial system does not continue into the New Covenant.

Circumcision was given to Abraham before it was incorporated in the Law of Moses, and Abraham and Jacob were circumcised. Paul had much to say about imposing the law of circumcision post Calvary, as I will write later.

The fact that something existed pre-Law, and also existed under the Law does not make it a post-Law requirement. Let us get beyond that fallacious thinking and false teaching, please.

II. GIVING FROM THE TIME OF MOSAIC LAW TO JESUS

The Mosaic Laws fall into three categories: the commandments; the ordinances; and the judgments.   Tithing fell into the category of ordinances and was legislated in Numbers 18.

Under the Mosaic Law required giving was legislated:

Leviticus 27:30-33	10%	Levite's Tithe
Deuteronomy 12:6-7	10%	Festival Tithe
Deuteronomy 14:28-29	10% (every 3rd year)	Poor Tithe

VOLUNTARY GIVING

The importance of voluntary offerings was not the percentage but the heart or attitude of the giver. Such offerings included first fruits gifts and freewill offerings.

The freewill offerings were given to the Levites but were shared with the poor and needy. Some references include:

> *"The Lord said to Moses 'Tell the people of Israel to bring me their sacred offerings. Accept the contributions from all whose hearts are moved to offer them."* Exodus 25:1

> *"Then you must celebrate the Festival of Harvest to honor the Lord your God. Bring him a freewill offering in proportion to the blessings you have received from Him."* Deuteronomy 16:10

> *"All must give as they are able, according to the blessings given to them by the Lord your God."* Deuteronomy 16:17

Examples of voluntary giving while under the Law can be found in: Exodus 25, 35:21-29; 36:5-6 Numbers 18:12; 1 Chronicles 29.

Voluntary giving always came from the heart.

I cannot ignore Malachi 3:8, the most often quoted tithing text in the Bible:

> *"Should people cheat God? Yet you have cheated me! But you ask, 'What do you mean? When did we ever cheat you?' You have cheated me of the tithes and offerings due to me."*

The message is clearly from God to His people, the nation of Israel. It is a message of love presented as a conversation between God and the priests and people of Israel through His prophet. The name "Malachi" means "My Messenger".

During the year 445 B. C. the Persian king permitted Nehemiah to return to Jerusalem to rebuild the wall following the rebuilding of the temple in 516 B.C. In 433 Nehemiah returned to the service of the Persian king.

After his absence the Jews fell once more into their old sin pattern. Tithes were withheld, the Israelites had intermarried, and the law was broken including the observance of the Sabbath. Malachi addresses these issues.

In Malachi 3:8, the prophet is speaking either to the Levitical priests or to the nation of Israel as a whole. In other words, it was referring either to the period before Nehemiah 10 – 13, and God was rebuking the priests for hoarding the tithe and neglecting the poor, or it was referring to a period long afterwards, and to the landowners who had stopped tithing and God was rebuking them. In all probability it was to the priests.

The term *"Tithes and offerings"* should be interpreted to mean tithes and heave offerings *("terumah" – Deuteronomy 12:6, 11, and 17)*. Therefore, this phrase means tithes from landowners and freewill heave offerings. Although the heave offerings were freewill (unsolicited) and primarily for the Levites, they were shared with the poor and needy. (This will be significant later as I write about Paul, the Law and the poor.)

The significance of the "heave" offerings instead of the tithe offerings is that the priests were robbing the poor and needy when they withheld a portion of these offerings.

Later in Malachi 3:10 the Jews are told to "bring all the tithes into the storehouse". The storehouse was a national reserve of food and sacrificial offerings maintained by the Levites.

These storehouses were part of the temple. Tithes were only food. The phrase *"that there may be food in my house"* means exactly what it says.

The entire context of Malachi is that of the Mosaic Law – the Old Covenant! As I will discuss next, Christians are not under the Mosaic Law, but under grace as presented in the New Testament.

III. GIVING FROM JESUS TO NOW

There are no references in the New Testament where God requires believers to give according to a predetermined percentage of income. However, tithing is referenced on three occasions:

1. Hebrews 7

2. Luke 18:9-14

3. Luke 11:41-42 (also recorded in Matthew 23:23)

Apart from recalling the tithe of Melchizedek in Hebrews, tithing is mentioned only critically. All of these references are in the context of Israel's obligation to God under the law and are not used in a prescriptive context to believers redeemed by Christ under the New Covenant.

Hebrews chapter 7:

Since this text is the only post-Calvary mention of tithing in the New Testament it must be completely understood.

(Information taken from NIV study Bible re: Author; Date; Recipients; and Theme.)

Author:
> There are three main candidates: Paul, Barnabas, and Apollos. From about 400 to 1600 A.D. the book was commonly called "The Epistle of Paul to the Hebrews".

The earliest suggested authorship is however Barnabas (A.D. 200), a coworker and close friend of Paul. Martin Luther later suggested Apollos, a name favored by many scholars today.

Date:

Clearly written after Christ and prior to the destruction of the temple in Jerusalem in A.D. 70.

Recipients:

Written to Jewish converts who were familiar with the Old Covenant and who were attempting to Judaize the gospel.

Theme:

No turning back to the old Jewish system. Jesus Christ is all in all – absolutely sufficient and supreme. It was written to prepare the Jewish Christians for life after the destruction of the temple and the termination of sacrifices and other Mosaic Law practices.

One significant purpose of Hebrews is to instruct the new first century Jewish Christians that they are no longer under the Old Covenant Law – The Mosaic Law, but rather the grace and power that comes through belief in Jesus Christ. The concern was that many Jewish Christians still considered themselves Jews and observed the Mosaic Law.

It was important to convince these new Christians that the Mosaic Law, the earthly city of Jerusalem, its temple, priesthood, and support structure were not a part of God's plan for His Church. They needed to stop paying tithes to the temple and stop supporting the Levitical priesthood. The temple was soon to be destroyed.

The word "tithe or tenth" is found in six verses of Hebrews 7 (2, 4, 5, 6, 8 and 9). These words do not appear elsewhere in the New Testament after Calvary.

In chapter 7 they refer either to Melchizedek and the tithe given by Abram (discussed earlier) or to the tithe required under Mosaic Law (vv. 5, 8 and 9).

In verses 5, 8 and 9 the action is referred to in the present tense *"are commanded in the law"*; *"tithes are paid"*; and *"the ones who collect the tithe"*, thus reflecting what was happening at the current time.

Hebrews 7:18 & 19 should end all discussion:

> *"Yes, the old requirement about the priesthood was set aside because it was weak and useless. For the law made nothing perfect, and now a better hope has taken its place. And that is how we draw near to God."*

Luke 18: 9 – 14

This is a parable about a Pharisee's prayer contrasted with that of a humble publican, in which the Pharisee boasts about tithing in v. 12:

> *"I fast twice a week, and I give you a tenth of my income."*

Much can be said about this parable, but for my purposes here, it is important to note that this was the status of the Jews prior to Calvary - they tithed under the Mosaic Law. Jesus set aside the law through His self-sacrifice.

Ephesians 2:14 – 16:

"For Christ himself has made peace between us Jews and you Gentiles by making us all one people. He has broken down the wall of hostility that used to separate us. By his death he ended the whole system of Jewish law that excluded the Gentiles. His purpose was to make peace between Jews and Gentiles by creating in himself one new person from the two groups. Together as one body, Christ reconciled both groups to God by means of his death, and our hostility toward each other was put to death."

This passage in Luke clearly does not teach tithing for Christians today but was a statement of the Pharisee's practice under the now abolished Mosaic Law.

Luke 11:41 – 42 and Matthew 23:23

"But how terrible it will be for you Pharisees! For you are careful to tithe even the tiniest part of your income, but you completely forget about justice and the love of God. You should tithe, yes, but you should not leave undone the more important things." Luke 11:42

"How terrible it will be for you teachers of religious law and you Pharisees. Hypocrites! For you are careful to tithe even the tiniest part of your income, but you ignore the important things of the law - justice, mercy, and faith. You should tithe, yes, but you should not leave undone the more important things." Matthew 23:23

Some teach that this proves Jesus validated the tithe for New Covenant believers, especially when coupled with the fact that Jesus did not teach against the tithe.

Jesus was born a Jew and reared as a Jew – under the jurisdiction of the Mosaic Law. The mention of the tithe in Luke 11 and Matthew 23 was in the context of the Old Covenant.

I am certain that Jesus lived his life in strict conformity with the Mosaic Law – He was sinless under the Law (in all probability Jesus did not tithe since He owned no land and produced nothing from the land).

> *"But when the right time came, God sent his Son, born of a woman, subject to the law.*
>
> *God sent him to buy freedom for us who were slaves to the law, so that he could adopt us as his very own children."* Galatians 4:4-5

When did the Old Covenant or Mosaic Law end and the New Covenant begin? At Calvary.

> *"Then Jesus shouted out again, and he gave up his spirit ('It is finished' - John 19:30).*
>
> *At that moment the curtain in the Temple was torn in two, from top to bottom. The earth shook, rocks split apart..."* Matthew 27:50-51

When the curtain in the Jerusalem Temple was torn from top to bottom the Most Holy Place was revealed to the world and the entire system of Jewish laws and ordinances ceased for those who accept Jesus as Savior – including the ordinance of the tithe.

That is all that the New Testament says about the tithe.

I therefore conclude that the tithe is not applicable to Christians after Calvary and it is never to be imposed on the believer in this dispensation any more than circumcision, animal sacrifices, and the Sabbath observance.

I am in good company with this conclusion as the apostle Paul, and ultimately the other apostles reached exactly the same conclusion.

Pay particular attention to what I am about to write. This is a "rubber hitting the road" statement, which I have never read nor heard made by any other Bible teacher. To me it seems obvious.

In the books of Acts and Galatians, Luke and Paul tell of a confrontation with the church leaders in Jerusalem over the Law, in which Paul prevailed.

"But some of the sect of the Pharisees who believed rose up, saying "It is necessary to circumcise them, and to command them to keep the Law of Moses." Acts 15:5

After the dust-up subsided the Apostles wrote:

"Since we have heard that some who went out from us have troubled you with words, unsettling your souls, saying "You must be circumcised and keep the law" – to whom we gave no such commandment –"Acts 15:24

And in Galatians 2:10 Paul writes:

"Their only suggestion was that we keep helping the poor, which I have always been eager to do."

Why did the other apostles request that Paul continue to remember the poor?

Because the tithe was eliminated and the tithe was the method the Jews had of caring for the poor.

Paul wrote further in his letter to the Galatians concerning the Law. When he wrote of the Law he often just wrote about circumcision as representative of the whole Law, since it was an easily recognizable, outward example of keeping the Law. One could substitute any requirement of the Law in place of circumcision. Such as animal sacrifices, the Sabbath, or tithing. For instance Galatians 5:6 could read:

*"For in Christ Jesus neither circumcision **(tithing)** nor uncircumcision **(not tithing)** has any value. The only thing that counts is faith expressing itself through love."*

Later Paul wrote about those who were requiring the new Gentile believers to comply with the Law:

"As for those agitators I wish they would go the whole way and emasculate themselves!" (v12)

Ok! Paul seems more than a little upset with the preachers of the Law to the New Testament believers.

If Paul wrote that to the first century preachers who were requiring believers to follow the Law, just imagine what he would write to the 21st century preachers who require the tithe … oh, I mean circumcision, or rather following any required law for salvation or for fellowship with Jesus.

With the clear elimination of the tithe, Paul and the other writers of the New Testament, never taught the tithe. Jesus never taught the tithe. History shows us that no early church leaders, whose writing we have (pre Council of Nicaea), ever wrote about the tithe.

The tithe did not actually enter into the New Covenant church until after the Council at Nicaea in 325 AD, when under

Constantine, it was instigated by the church as a way of paying for the emerging and growing group of professional church leaders.

Most historians usually agree that the tithe did not come into prominence until after A.D. 567, when the Council of Tours put forth decrees for tithing and some form of enforcement began. Eventually the Roman Catholic Church went on to not only collect the tithe, but to vehemently enforce its payment, and sell other things; such as indulgencies, and the administration of last rites, in order to put even more money into their greedy little pockets.

As long as the professional clergy could keep people ignorant of the truth of God's Word, they could profit from it. Sadly, this sounds a little like some of our churches in America today, doesn't it.

Does this mean that we are no longer to give to the church? Of course not! What it means is that the decision to spend God's resources on buying a car, taking a vacation, going out to dinner, or buying that new dress is just as important as what you drop into the church collection box.

Every spending decision involves God's money and is therefore a spiritual decision. We as Christians are held to a higher standard – acknowledging first that we belong to God and then that God is sovereign over all that we are and have.

What we find is that almost every doctrine of the Old Testament is perfected in the New Testament, or said another way, almost every doctrine of the New Testament is anticipated in the Old Testament.

The doctrine of giving is no exception.

Apart from God the Old Testament Scriptures have no status – they derive their authority from God. Jesus, who is God, took upon Himself that authority in the New Testament. What the Law pointed to, came in the person of Jesus Christ. Jesus taught with authority.

We are given some of the teachings of Jesus in Matthew 5, 6 &7. Some simply refer to these passages as "the beatitudes" (sometimes poorly translated as "happy" or "blessed"). The real theme of these chapters is the kingdom of heaven, and in His teaching Jesus turns the teaching of The Law "outside in".

What do I mean by that? This is where the rubber really hits the road. God came to earth to communicate with man, eyeball to eyeball, some important messages about Himself.

Jesus taught that The Law was concerned about outward actions but that He, God, was concerned about inward desires. One could commit murder without killing anyone, or commit adultery without actually having sex. The action, or sin, was first in the heart before, or if, it ever became an action.

Now listen to this … the act of giving to God occurs first in the heart of a believer/giver before, or if, it ever becomes an action. The amount of the gift must be determined "in the heart". The intent of the heart must be that of love.

So, you can lay to rest the "legalistic tithe", giving out of compulsion or following some formula, the "prosperity gospel", giving out of a desire to personally benefit, or any other doctrine of giving that you want to invent.

It is grace giving from the heart of a believer out of love for God and obedience to the leading of the Holy Spirit (God) …. Period.

That is exactly why Jesus said in these passages: *"For where your treasure is, there your heart will be also."* Matthew 6:21.

Jesus also taught about stewardship using parables. The Greek word *"oikonomos"* appears two times in His parables. Once in the parable of the servants found in Luke12:42 – 48, and again in Luke 16:1-13. On both occasions it is translated "manager". One who is in charge of an owner's household or estate.

One day we will each account to the Owner as to how we used His property... all of it. That 10% that you gave, whether it be of your pre-tax or after-tax earnings, will not excuse or justify your use of the other 90%. (By the way, statistics indicate that per tax returns, those who claim to be Christian give an average of 1.7% of their adjusted gross income to charity).

> *"So why do you condemn another Christian? Why do you look down on another Christian? Remember, each of us will stand personally before the judgment seat of God. For the Scriptures say, 'As surely as I live,' says the Lord, 'every knee will bow to me and every tongue will confess allegiance to God.' Yes, each of us will have to give a personal account to God."* Romans 14:10-12

I believe that if we are seeking God's purposes for using His resources, we will soon be surpassing the 1.7% average and yes, even the 10% of pre-tax earnings benchmark that so many preachers teach as God's commandment as to giving.

Actually the amount of our giving is **NOT** important to God. After all He doesn't need any more money. He already owns everything. It is however important to us. It is part of our testimony.

That's why giving, because of some perceived obligation or guilt-trip brought on by a TV evangelist or others is ineffectual.

Too many donations are extracted by effective speakers who can produce pity in an audience. Pity, not just for those in need or some cause, but for the God Who wants to help but just can't due to His lack of money. Donors are moved to help remove God (and the speaker) from this embarrassing situation He has gotten Himself into.

God said:

> *"You must each make up your own mind as to how much you should give. Don't give reluctantly or in response to pressure. For God loves the person who gives cheerfully."* 2 Corinthians 9:7

Also, if you are giving because someone told you that God would pay you back many times over with material wealth, you too are wrong.

> *"Oh, what a wonderful God we have! How great are his riches and wisdom and knowledge! How impossible it is for us to understand his decisions and his methods! For who can know what the lord is thinking? Who knows enough to be his counselor? And who could ever give him so much that he would have to pay it back? For everything comes from him; everything exists by his power and is intended for his glory. To him be glory evermore. Amen."* Romans 11:33-36

But read this:

> *"Honor the Lord with your wealth and with the best part of everything your land produces. Then he will fill your barns with grain, and your vats will overflow with the finest wine."* Proverbs 3:9-10

"It is possible to give freely and become wealthier, but those who are stingy will lose everything. The generous prosper and are satisfied; those who refresh others will themselves be refreshed." Proverbs 11:24-25

"'Bring all the tithes into the storehouse so there will be enough food in my Temple. If you do,' says the Lord Almighty, 'I will open the windows of heaven for you. I will pour out a blessing so great you won't have enough room to take it in! Try it! Let me prove it to you!'" Malachi 3:10

"If you give, you will receive. Your gift will return to you in full measure, pressed down, shaken together to make room for more, and running over. Whatever measure you use in giving-large or small-it will be used to measure what is given back to you." Luke 6:38

But now this:

"Jesus watched him go and then said to his disciples, 'How hard it is for rich people to get into the Kingdom of God! It is easier for a camel to go through the eye of a needle than for a rich person to enter the Kingdom of God!'" Luke 18:24-25

"Yet true religion with contentment is great wealth. After all, we didn't bring anything with us when we came into the world, and we certainly cannot carry anything with us when we die. So if we have enough food and clothing, let us be content.

But people who long to be rich fall into temptation and are trapped by many foolish and harmful desires that plunge them into ruin and destruction. For the love of money is at the root of all kinds of evil. And some people, craving money, have wandered from the faith and pierced themselves with many sorrows.

But you, Timothy, belong to God; so run from all these evil things, and follow what is right and good. Pursue a godly life, along with faith, love, perseverance, and gentleness. Fight the good fight for what we believe. Hold tightly to the eternal life that God has given you, which you have confessed so well before many witnesses.

And I command you before God, who gives life to all, and before Christ Jesus, who gave a good testimony before Pontius Pilate, that you obey his commands with all purity. Then no one can find fault with you from now until our Lord Jesus Christ returns." 1Timothy 6:6-14

"Tell those who are rich in this world not to be proud and not to trust in their money, which will soon be gone. But their trust should be in the living God, who richly gives us all we need for our enjoyment. Tell them to use their money to do good. They should be rich in good works and should give generously to those in need, always being ready to share with others whatever God has given them. By doing this they will be storing up their treasure as a good foundation for the future so that they may take hold of real life." 1Timothy 6:17-19

Is there some conflict here? No!

"Unless you are faithful in small matters, you won't be faithful in large ones. If you cheat even a little, you won't be honest with greater responsibilities. And if you are untrustworthy about worldly wealth, who will trust you with the true riches of heaven? And if you are not faithful with other people's money, why should you be trusted with money of your own? No one can serve two masters. For you will hate one and love the other, or be devoted to one and despise the other. You cannot serve both God and money." Luke 16:10-13

"And even when you do ask, you don't get it because your whole motive is wrong-you want only what will give you pleasure. You adulterers! Don't you realize that friendship with this world makes you an enemy of God? I say it again, that if your aim is to enjoy this world, you can't be a friend of God." James 4:3-4

Earthly wealth is perhaps more of a test and an obligation than a blessing. Maybe the prosperity God talks about is other than on earth.

"Don't store up treasures here on earth, where they can be eaten by moths and get rusty, and where thieves break in and steal.

Store your treasures in heaven, where they will never become moth-eaten or rusty and where they will be safe from thieves. Wherever your treasure is, there your heart and thoughts will also be.

Your eye is a lamp for your body. A pure eye lets sunshine into your soul. But an evil eye shuts out the light and plunges you into darkness. If the light you think you have is really darkness, how deep that darkness will be!

No one can serve two masters. For you will hate one and love the other, or be devoted to one and despise the other. You cannot serve both God and money.

So I tell you, don't worry about everyday life-whether you have enough food, drink, and clothes. Doesn't life consist of more than food and clothing? Look at the birds. They don't need to plant or harvest or put food in barns because your heavenly Father feeds them. And you are far more valuable to him than they are. Can all your worries add a single moment to your life? Of course not.

And why worry about your clothes? Look at the lilies and how they grow. They don't work or make their clothing, yet Solomon in all his glory was not dressed as beautifully as they are. And if God cares so wonderfully for flowers that are here today and gone tomorrow, won't he more surely care for you?

You have so little faith!

So don't worry about having enough food or drink or clothing. Why be like the pagans who are so deeply concerned about these things? Your heavenly Father already knows all your needs, and he will give you all you need from day to day if you live for him and make the Kingdom of God your primary concern.

So don't worry about tomorrow, for tomorrow will bring its own worries. Today's trouble is enough for today. Matthew 6:19-34

Prosperity is God fulfilling His purposes through your life. He wants us to prosper in Him. Do your work as a testimony to God. Allow God to determine your circumstances, including your earthly wealth. Your prosperity will be in glory! This is God's plan.

"This 'foolish' plan of God is far wiser than the wisest of human plans, and God's weakness is far stronger than the greatest of human strength.

Remember, dear brothers and sisters, that few of you were wise in the world's eyes, or powerful, or wealthy when God called you. Instead, God deliberately chose things the world considers foolish in order to shame those who think they are wise. And he chose those who are powerless to shame those who are powerful. God chose things despised by the world, things counted as nothing at all, and used them to bring to nothing what the world considers important, so that no one can ever boast in the presence of God.

God alone made it possible for you to be in Christ Jesus. For our benefit God made Christ to be wisdom itself. He is the one who made us acceptable to God. He made us pure and holy, and he gave himself to purchase our freedom. As the Scriptures say, ' The person who wishes to boast should boast only of what the Lord has done.'" 1 Corinthians 1:25-31

Our giving expresses the condition of our heart, our testimony, our love of God, and our attitude toward God and toward the world. Anyone who gives willingly and with true love will be blessed by God. God will honor our heart and not the amount of our gift.

"Jesus went over to the collection box in the Temple and sat and watched as the crowds dropped in their money. Many rich people put in large amounts. Then a poor widow came and dropped in two pennies. He called his disciples to him and said, 'I assure you, this poor widow has given more than all the others have given. For they gave a tiny part of their surplus, but she, poor as she is, has given everything she has.'" Mark 12:41-44

THE NEW TESTAMENT TEACHES US MUCH ABOUT GIVING. LET ME SHARE TWO THINGS.

1.   The New Testament says that giving should be:

A. Personal. 2 Corinthians 9:7a
   "You must each make up your own mind as to how much you should give."

B. Cheerful.   2 Corinthians 9:7b
   "Don't give reluctantly or in response to pressure. For God loves the person who gives cheerfully."

C. Proportional. 2 Corinthians 8:11b-12

"Give whatever you can according to what you have. If you are really eager to give, it isn't important how much you are able to give. God wants you to give what you have, not what you don't have."

D. Regular. 1 Corinthians 16:2a
"On every Lord's Day, each of you should put aside some amount of money in relation to what you have earned and save it for this offering. Don't wait until I get there and then try to collect it all at once."

E. Sacrificial. 2 Corinthians 8:2 – 3
"Though they have been going through much trouble and hard times, their wonderful joy and deep poverty have overflowed in rich generosity."

2.   The New Testament teaches giving through several parables, including the following:

The parable of the shrewd manager (Luke 16: 1–13):

"Jesus told this story to his disciples: 'A rich man hired a manager to handle his affairs, but soon a rumor went around that the manager was thoroughly dishonest. So his employer called him in and said, 'What's this I hear about your stealing from me? Get your report in order, because you are going to be dismissed.'

The manager thought to himself, 'Now what? I'm through here, and I don't have the strength to go out and dig ditches, and I'm too proud to beg. I know just the thing! And then I'll have plenty of friends to take care of me when I leave!'

So he invited each person who owed money to his employer to come and discuss the situation. He asked the first one, 'How much do you owe him?'

The man replied, 'I owe him eight hundred gallons of olive oil.' So the manager told him, 'Tear up that bill and write another one for four hundred gallons.'

'And how much do you owe my employer?' he asked the next man. 'A thousand bushels of wheat'' was the reply. 'Here,' the manager said, 'take your bill and replace it with one for only eight hundred bushels.'

The rich man had to admire the dishonest rascal for being so shrewd. And it is true that the citizens of this world are more shrewd than the godly are. I tell you, use your worldly resources to benefit others and make friends. In this way, your generosity stores up a reward for you in heaven.

Unless you are faithful in small matters, you won't be faithful in large ones. If you cheat even a little, you won't be honest with greater responsibilities.

And if you are untrustworthy about worldly wealth, who will trust you with the true riches of heaven? And if you are not faithful with other people's money, why should you be trusted with money of your own? No one can serve two masters. For you will hate one and love the other, or be devoted to one and despise the other. You cannot serve both God and money."

The lesson is: use what is not yours and you cannot keep to build up treasure for eternity. You can't take it with you but you can send it on ahead.

This is important when trying to determine how much to give – what is sacrificial. The question really becomes "How much do you want to consume on earth, or leave behind, and how much treasure do you want to build for eternity". It's a matter of being shrewd!

As Jim Elliot, the slain missionary once said: "He is no fool who gives what he cannot keep to gain what he cannot lose."

The Parables of the Hidden Treasure and the Pearl from Matthew 13:44-46 (NIV):

"The kingdom of heaven is like treasure hidden in a field. When a man found it, he hid it again, and then in his joy went and sold all he had and bought that field. Again, the kingdom of heaven is like a merchant looking for fine pearls. When he found one of great value, he went away and sold everything he had and bought it."

Randy Alcorn in his little book *"The Treasure Principle"* gave a great illustration about a first-century Hebrew and used Matthew 13:44 as his basis for the illustration. Here's my story, let's call it the OC (that's Orange County California) version.

Bob was 25, had his MBA from USC and was on the move professionally in his new position with the Irvine Company. He had all the toys and the debt to go with them. He enjoyed the OC restaurants, social scene and dreamed of the ocean view place on the bluff in his future.

Bob liked to stay physically fit so he tried to jog a few miles each morning. On this particular March morning as he jogged his way through the streets down to the beach, the morning fog had severely limited his vision. He decided to cut the jog short and took a short-cut down a canyon path that he had never run. As he dashed down this strange new path, he tripped on something and went flying to the ground. As he felt around to locate the object that had caused his fall, his hand pressed upon a handle of some sort. As he pulled on the handle, the canyon side to his left began to open exposing a huge cavernous space.

As Bob felt his way through the fog and entered the now exposed cave his vision was captured by the limited light reflecting off of several shinny objects. Upon closer inspection, he discovered these objects to be made of gold, platinum, silver, diamonds and other precious gems. The cave was massive and was filled with these valuable objects.

Being a USC business major he quickly began to calculate the value – it was enormous. From just the first 20 feet Bob's estimate was well over a billion dollars – the space was easily one hundred times that big. This was a tremendous find! How had it gotten here and more importantly – who owned it?

As his mind raced, Bob concluded that it must have been hidden in these hills for a long time, perhaps for hundreds of years. Maybe no one alive today knew about this immense treasure.

Quickly Bob left the cave, threw back the lever, thus closing the cave entrance, hid the lever beneath a pile of stones, and set off for his condo – at a much quicker pace. He now did not seem to even notice the chill and fog as his mind raced with the beginning of a plan.

Through his mastery of the internet he soon discovered that the owner of the five acre parcel had inherited the property ten years earlier. The man now lived in Wisconsin – he couldn't be too bright Bob reasoned.

After weeks of intense negotiation (Bob had taken a class on negotiation at USC) he had reached an agreement to purchase the property. It was going to cost him $500,000! An large sum for an unusable five acres at the bottom of the canyon – but a real bargain considering the treasure that was hidden there. The agreement called for Bob to pay the seller 10% of the purchase price each year for ten years.

Bob's superior negotiation skills had arranged for the buyout to be interest free, however if he missed an annual payment he forfeited the right to own the land. He could not take possession or transfer ownership until the full purchase price had been fully paid.

Bob was not happy with this arrangement, but he had gotten himself into such debt, what with the BMW and other toys that he had no ability to borrow from any financial institution to purchase what appeared to others as an overpriced asset.

Bob decided that somehow he would have his fortune much sooner than ten years. He began selling off the toys. He moved into a single room he rented in the house of a San Clemente home owner – it was still OC however fringe OC. More importantly, it was cheap and Bob was now interested in cheap. Instead of replacing the BMW he took the bus. No more $200 dinners at the best restaurants or trips to Napa. No, Bob took on extra jobs, whatever he could find. He was determined to own that property as quickly as possible.

His friends were certain Bob had lost it, and they soon abandoned him. The strange thing about Bob was that he seemed to be enjoying this new lifestyle. He even acted joyful as he paid out all he could to purchase this seemingly worthless land.

A few of his fellow MBA's pointed out to Bob that he was only legally required to pay 10% a year, and not everything he earned. Some even reported observing Bob laughing to himself as he jogged each morning along the beach – how very strange.

From the moment of his discovery, Bob's life changed. His very paradigm shifted radically and he was consumed with the thought of owning "The Treasure" – becoming the richest man in OC – perhaps all of the world. Everything he did, every dollar he spent was now measured against the possibility of owning this treasure one day sooner.

The Apostle John gives us a very small glimpse of the treasure that awaits us in heaven, when in Revelations he described the New Jerusalem:

Revelations 21:18 -21

"The construction of its wall was of Jasper; and the city was pure gold, like clear glass. The foundations of the wall of the city were adorned with all kinds of precious stones; the first foundation was jasper, the second sapphire, the third chalcedony, the fourth emerald, the fifth sardonyx, the eight beryl, the ninth topaz, the tenth chrysoprase, the eleventh jacinth, and the twelfth amethyst. The twelve gates were twelve pearls; each individual gate was of one pearl. And the street of the city was pure gold, like transparent glass."

Far greater wealth than was discovered by Bob in my little fictitious story above. Jesus captured this story in a few short sentences in the two parables quoted above.

The word "joy" is important in His describing the attitude of the finder of the treasure as he sold everything to purchase it. That is the same attitude God describes should be ours as we give to store up treasure in heaven for eternity. If we truly captured this thought, our paradigm would shift. Ten percent would never enter our minds as an option. Sacrifice would be joyful - even hilarious. We may even be caught laughing as we joyously jog the beach.

Why do I continue to disparage the "legalistic tithe"? Because even more than the "prosperity gospel", the tithe robs Christians of the joy of giving. Although wrong, those giving into the prosperity gospel have the anticipation of obtaining health and wealth. It is "kinda" like buying a lottery ticket. You don't really think that you are going to win the big jackpot but for two dollars you purchase the chance to win it. As long as some chance exists you can dream of how you will spend all of that money. Therefore giving under the prosperity gospel is buying a dream of wealth. There is always a chance you could win it.

Whereas, some who give the tithe, pay it like they do their house payment. It is a requirement they believe, and they give the tithe reluctantly, or grudgingly, or out of compulsion, or fear of God's punishment if they don't give it.

No joy there, not even the anticipation of "winning" anything. Certainly not what the Apostle Paul said should be our motivation.

Many of us sung about this "joy" around a campfire in our youth. I sung it often as an RA. The song was written by George William Cooke in 1925. Here are a few of its lyrics.

> I have the joy, joy, joy, joy.
> Down in my heart. Down in my heart. Down in my heart.
> I have the joy, joy, joy, joy.
> Down in my heart.
> Down in my heart to stay

A person receives this "joy" through grace giving.

Ben Gill was the Chairman and CEO of Resources Services, Inc. (RSI) based in Dallas, Texas. I had the privilege of working alongside RSI several times to assist in capital campaigns at mega churches. During 2017 RSI linked up with Generis, and combined they have helped to raise over ten billion dollars for over ten thousand churches over a forty year period.

Ben wrote a book in 1994 titled *"The Joy of Giving"*. This is some of what he wrote:

"My life has been spent helping people learn the gift of giving. After twenty-five years in this pursuit, I come now to tell you that one fact has become increasingly clear: the happiest people on earth are the people who have learned the joy of giving."[xvii]

I submitted an early draft of this book to a close personal friend for his review and critique. My friend was a professor at a Christian University until he recently retired. Obviously I respect this person greatly or I would not have asked for his thoughts.

Actually, he is probably the most Godly man that I have been privileged to know. And that says a lot since I have known many of today's Christian leaders.

Let me share one experience that I had with the Professor and his wife (let's name her Rita). I wrote earlier that my wife's father, Jim, was living with us in Yorba Linda at the age of eighty six and legally blind. Jim was near the end of his life. As a matter of fact, the doctors had given him no more than six months to live. What I did not write earlier was that Jim was not a Christian. When Suzanne had first witnessed to him thirty years earlier, Jim told her to leave his home and never come back.

In spite of this rebuke, we continued to pray for Jim's salvation and Suzanne witnessed to him every opportunity she could, but he was just not open to hearing the gospel. A stubborn man with a strong German ancestry.

When Suzanne shared Jim's situation with the Professor and his wife, they began to pray with us concerning Jim's salvation. As it turns out Rita, a committed evangelist, was from Germany. She determined to use this common ancestry to build a relationship with Jim. Over time she built such a relationship.

One evening the Professor and Rita drove to our home in Yorba Linda for dinner, but really so that Rita could share the gospel with Jim - one on one. After dinner we all left the room except Jim and Rita. Rita shared her heart and the gospel with Jim. He prayed to receive Jesus.

The Professor and his wife gave of their time, their ability to share God's Word, and their ancestry so that one blind stubborn old man, who was about to die, would hear the gospel in his cultural dialect and secure his eternity with Jesus. My friend and his wife gave from their hearts as led by the Holy Spirit.

After reading my book manuscript, the Professor called to tell me that he anguished over my depiction of the tithe. He said that for all of his Christian life, and he is over 80, he has tithed.

He shared that he always thought that to tithe was an important part of his Christian walk. After reading my argument against teaching the tithe, he told me that in the end he had to agree with me, reluctantly. He also shared that he regularly gives thirty percent of his income as his "tithe".

I now understood that I must pause, and dwell a little more on the subject of tithing, and the Christian walk.

I wrote earlier: *"It is important to note that tithing as a part of a giving discipline is not wrong in itself, in fact it can be a very useful and practical part of a believers giving convictions."*

Randy Alcorn, in his book *"Money Possessions and Eternity"* called tithing *"the training wheels of giving"*.

He went on to write:

"The tithe is God's historical method to get people on the path of giving. In that sense, it can serve as a gateway to the joy of true "grace giving" today, just as it gave rise to the spontaneous, joyous, freewill giving we see in various Old Testament passages. It's unhealthy to view tithing as a place to stop with our giving, but it can still be a good place to start."[xviii]

Mr. David Green, the founder and owner of the Hobby Lobby stores, wrote a book titled *"Giving it all Away"* in which he writes the following story:

"My journey begins in the cotton fields of my youth, learning the importance of tithing. I count myself fortunate to have received this message early and consistently from my parents. I was taught to give

God ten percent. Our family took Jesus literally when he said, 'It is more blessed to give than to receive' (Acts 20:35).

My mother was particularly devoted to tithing. I remember when someone from the church brought our family some food – say a bag of potatoes or some corn – Mother immediately calculated the market value of the gift so she could tithe ten percent."[xix]

"Today we've landed on giving roughly 50 percent of our profits. But we continue to pray and rely on the Holy Spirit for guidance."[xx]

The annual profit for Hobby Lobby stores is unknown to me, but I have been told that it exceeds one billion dollars. Mr. Green has moved far beyond the tithe, but apparently that is where he began his giving. A 2019 article in Forbes magazine states that the Green family is the largest donor to Christian organizations in the world.

I have been privileged to work with Mr. Green, not personally but through his organization, on several projects where he has purchased real estate property to donate to Christian ministries and churches. One such property involved Mariners Church.

I first became aware of Mr. Green through Jerry Falwell, when during 2004 the Green family trust purchased a vacant Ericsson cellphone plant in Lynchburg, Va., for $10.5 million and donated it a year later to Jerry Falwell's Liberty University. The property contained one million square feet under roof.

One recipient of a real estate property donation from Mr. Green was a prominent Baptist church where Suzanne and I worshiped for about eight years. The Senior Pastor of that church consistently taught the tithe as a requirement for the Christian life. However, this pastor shared that his professor at Dallas Theological Seminary, Dr. Howard Hendricks, taught his students to not teach tithing.

I was told that Dr. Hendricks taught that if one felt compelled to teach percentage giving, teach a percentage other than 10%. Use 9% or use 11%, or teach any percentage other than 10%. He seems to agree with the teaching of Thomas Aquinas (1250 AD):

"Paying tithes, it appears, is no longer of precept, because the precept to pay tithes was given in the Old Law. . . . Paying tithes cannot be considered a moral precept, however, because natural reason does not dictate that one ought to give a tenth, rather than a ninth or an eleventh. Therefore, it is a ceremonial or a judicial precept." Thomas Aquinas, *Summa Theologiæ*, vol. 39 (New York: McGraw-Hill, 1964), 139.

Why? Too much baggage, misconception, and false teaching associated with the ten percent. If a person gives a percentage other than ten percent, they cannot call it a tithe, as the word tithe means a tenth. So all of that legalistic baggage disappears if you don't call it a tithe.

"For over fifty years, Howard G. Hendricks was a professor at Dallas Theological Seminary, where he taught "Bible Exposition and Hermeneutics" to freshmen. He mentored many Christian leaders, including Chuck Swindoll, Tony Evans, Joseph Stowell Robert Jeffress and David Jeremiah."[xxi]

So which is it? Is tithing bad theology or is it good theology? Should believers tithe or should they not tithe? As I wrote earlier:

"The problem arises when it [tithing] is taught as a commandment [or a requirement], and as the beginning and end of God's acceptable standard today. Teaching such a doctrine is simply inaccurate."

The bottom line is, in my humble opinion, if tithing is viewed in the proper perspective, and is part of an overall discipline of giving, coupled with praying and relying on the Holy Spirit for guidance, it can be a good and acceptable part of a Christian's walk with God. If tithing is taught and followed as a method of placing God first in our lives and in our stewardship, it is good, right and proper.

But, there is nothing special about ten percent, except that it is easy to multiply by ten percent. We can put God first with any percentage as long as we do it with a pure heart. The important issue is to view all that we have as God's property and not as our property.

The tithe unfortunately gets entwined with legalism, and is misrepresented by some who teach it. So I say, why not teach and practice giving as Jesus taught giving, as the Apostle Paul taught giving, or as Dr. Howard Hendricks taught giving?

Give consistently and proportionally, but multiply your income by 9% or 11% or any other percentage other than 10%, to arrive at the gift amount. Do not call it a tithe. The word "offering" comes to my mind. As seen above, Mr. Green gives at the 50% level and the Professor at the 30% level, but more importantly, they have both committed everything to God.

I wrote earlier about John Wesley, who was used of God to start the Methodist Church. I also wrote that he was perhaps the greatest preacher of the eighteenth century, but what I did not write earlier was that John Wesley made enormous amounts of money from his writings and speaking.

Mr. Wesley was not always so wealthy. In fact, he knew great poverty as a child. His father was the Anglican priest in one of England's lowest-paying parishes. He had nine children to support and was rarely out of debt. Once John witnessed his father being marched off to debtor's prison.

What does John Wesley have to teach us about giving and about the tithe?

While teaching at Oxford, an incident changed John Wesley's perspective on money. He had just purchased some pictures for his room when an old woman came to his door. It was a bitter cold winter day, and she had nothing to protect herself from such cold. Wesley looked about his apartment to give her some money to buy a coat but found he had too little left. He felt great guilt about the way he had spent his money on pictures, and vowed that it would not happen again.

Wesley began to limit his expenses so that he would have more money to give to the poor. He records that one year his income was 30 pounds and his living expenses 28 pounds, so he had 2 pounds to give away (not a tithe). The next year his income doubled, but he still managed to live on 28 pounds, so he had 32 pounds to give to the poor. In the third year, his income jumped to 90 pounds, and in the fourth year to 120 pounds, but he continued to live on 28 pounds and give away the surplus.

John Wesley believed that the Christian should not tithe, but give away all extra income once the personal expenses of life were paid. With increasing income, what should rise was not the Christian's standard of living, but the standard of giving.

Keep your heart open to the leading of the Holy Spirit.

"Do you not know that God entrusted you with that money (all above what buys necessities for your families) to feed the hungry, to clothe the naked, to help the stranger, the widow, the fatherless; and, indeed, as far as it will go, to relieve the wants of all mankind? How can you, how dare you, defraud the Lord, by applying it to any other purpose?"
— John Wesley

THE STEWARD'S HEART

Wherever I have experienced the teaching of God's principles of stewardship, hearts have been changed and donations of time, talent and money to God's ministries have increased dramatically. It is truly all about the heart of a believer.

What do I mean when I say "the heart" of a believer? What does the Bible mean when it speaks of "the heart"?

My wife, Suzanne, enjoys watching Hallmark movies and invariably they are about the heart. When these movies refer to the heart it is about emotions such as love, compassion, sadness or joy. But that is not what the Bible refers to when it speaks of the heart.

If you search the internet for "heart", "mind" and "Bible" you will get hundreds of verses about the heart which are spread throughout the Bible. One thing that this says to us is that the believer's heart is important to God. But is it a fourth dimension to our creation, with body, soul and spirit being the other three dimensions?

I think not. I believe that the heart brings together the three dimensions to form our emotions, our thinking, our will and our conscience. It is the center of our beliefs.

Now you may readily agree that the heart encompasses our emotions. That's right out of Hallmark movies. But our thinking? Matthew 9:4:

But Jesus, knowing their thoughts, said "Why do you think evil in your hearts?"

"But Mary kept all these things and pondered them in her heart." Matthew 2:19

Jesus said that thinking took place in the heart and not just the brain.

Our will? Acts 11:23:

*"When he came and had seen the grace of God, he was glad, and encouraged them all that with **purpose of heart** they should continue with the Lord."*

As to conscience, the apostle John wrote in 1 John 3:19 -20:

"And by this we know that we are of the truth, and shall assure our hearts before Him. For if our heart condemns us, God is greater than our heart, and knows all things."

The words "assure" and "condemn" refer to things of the conscience. There are other places that indicate that our conscience is part of our heart, such as Hebrews 10:22:

"Let us draw near with a true heart in full assurance of faith, having our hearts sprinkled from an evil conscience and our bodies washed with pure water."

The Bible teaches that the heart does not just feel emotions but also thinks, determines right from wrong and sets the direction of our life. You could say that the heart is the window of our whole life. Or, to put it another way, it is the center of a person. God exposes our hearts in many ways.

Take the story of Abraham and Isaac. By the act of his intent to sacrifice Isaac in obedience to God, the heart of Abraham was revealed. Isaac was the love of his life and he was willing to give him up for God.

The rich young ruler was not willing to give up the love of his life, his riches and possessions, to accept Jesus. His heart was revealed by Jesus. I am sure the young man would have given 10% or perhaps even 50%, but 100%? No way. That is why Jesus asked for 100%. To reveal his true heart.

When Jesus taught the beatitudes to a crowd on a mountain in Galilee, He was teaching about the heart. He spoke about the law and then contrasted how it was now all about the heart. And He said: *"Blessed are the pure in heart, for they shall see God."* Matthew 5:8.

God was not speaking of a person's emotions but of the purity of a person. A person must be pure to fellowship with, or to see God. *"Pursue peace with all people, and holiness, without which no one will see the Lord"* Hebrews 12:14.

To see a holy God, one must have purity of heart. *"Who may ascend into the hill of the Lord? "Or who may stand in His holy place? He who has clean hands and a pure heart."* Psalm 24:3&4

How do we obtain a pure heart? Earlier I mentioned my pastor from Lemon Grove, Bob Kleinschmidt (or Brother Bob as we addressed him). Bro. Bob taught me that we have two relationships with God. An eternal relationship which we gain through salvation, this relationship is never broken, and a temporal relationship, called fellowship, which we enter into only when our hearts are pure. To gain this purity of heart we must confess ours sins and receive His forgiveness.

"If we confess our sins, He is faithful and just to forgive our sins and to cleanse us from all unrighteousness." 1 John 1:9.

This is the very key to our giving. When we give of our time, talent and treasure it must always be with a pure heart.

This pierces into our inner being, into our very thoughts and intentions. No more following the rules outwardly as under the law. When we give, God sees all of this. Whatever we give, it must be with purity of heart.

To open your heart to Jesus, you must make a conscious decision to give God full control of your life, as your Lord as well as your savior. That means to cease living for your own self-interest. To do this is a life-changing experience.

After you do this, discerning God's will for your giving requires a renewed mind: *"Do not be conformed to this world, but be transformed by the renewal of your mind, that by testing you may discern what is the will of God, what is good and acceptable."* Romans 12:2.

In order to determine what God wants for you to be, do, say or give you must spend time reading His Word. It is the primary way that God leads us. *"Your Word is a lamp to my feet and a light for my path"* Psalm 119:105

Christians also have prayer and the Holy Spirit to guide our hearts in determining God's will for our actions.

One thing you can count on … at some point in your life you will have to make a decision that will reveal your heart toward God. This is usually a decision about giving … your time, your talent, and your money.

There can be no doubt that this possessive clinging to things is one of the most harmful habits in the [Christian] life. Because it is so natural, it is rarely recognized for the evil that it is. But it's out workings are tragic. – A. W. Tozer

MINISTRIES AND GIFTS

I cannot conclude without discussing how the Church and other Christian ministries should solicit and value the gifts they receive. By way of illustration, let me tell you a story about coffee.

I enjoy drinking coffee. I mean, I really, really enjoy drinking coffee. I began in the US Navy during 1963 and I have since consumed quite a lot of coffee during my long life.

When my wife, family and I went into missions with the Southern Baptists, we were assigned to Peru. However, before getting to Peru we had to undergo a year of Spanish language study in Costa Rica. Costa Rica had great coffee! But even better than that, we lived next to a coffee plantation. On the other side of that plantation was a coffee roasting factory. The smell was terrific to a coffee lover.

Quite often, I would walk through the coffee plants to the roasting factory and purchase fresh roasted coffee beans. I would take those roasted beans, grind them into grounds and make coffee one cup at a time. It was tremendous.

Then we got to Peru.

It seemed that I would never find a great, or even a decent cup of coffee in Peru. But I kept trying. One evening while out to dinner, the waiter asked if I wanted coffee after my meal. Never giving up I said "of course".

Actually I said "por supuesto".

The waiter brought a small beat-up tin cup to my table and set it down. I asked, "What is that?" The waiter said it contained the essence of coffee. Still puzzled I asked, "And what do I do with this essence of coffee?"

The answer was to mix the essence with hot water in an amount depending upon the strength of coffee that you want. So I mixed it 50/50. It was strong but not bitter, and it tasted great. I continued to frequent that restaurant and was soon just telling the waiter to heat up the essence and I drank it without mixing in water. Strong, not bitter and great tasting.

We left Peru to return to California before I ever asked how to make the essence of coffee. That was in December 1980.

For almost twenty years I tried everything and every type of coffee machine to duplicate that essence. I failed and I finally just gave up. During the year 2000 I joined the staff at Shadow Mountain Community Church and soon ran into some old friends we had known prior to going to Peru. Jack and Linda Miller asked us to join them for dinner. After dinner Linda asked if I wanted coffee. Of course I did, but I told Linda that I was sure, given the late hour, that I would be the only one wanting coffee and therefore not to make a pot of coffee just for me. "Oh no", she said. "I prepared in advance the essence of coffee and I serve it one cup at a time. Depending upon how strong you want it, I just mix it with hot water." Now that was intriguing, so I said "Mix it half and half".

Eureka! That was truly it. The essence of coffee.

Immediately I inquired as to how to make the essence. I was told that it required a special apparatus that she had purchased from a local coffee shop. The next morning I was at the coffee shop when it opened. I purchased the apparatus.

The process surprised me. First you dump a full pound of coffee grounds into the filter. The better the coffee grounds the better the final product. Then you put cold water over the coffee grounds and let it sit for at least 24 hours. Yes, I said "cold water".

You pull the plug beneath the filter and allow the water to seep through the thick filter until the pot, which only holds about 24 ounces is full. This takes a long while, but that's it. You can then mix this liquid, the essence of coffee, with hot water to make the most delicious cup of coffee you've ever tasted.

The essence must be refrigerated and even then it will only last about one week. Drink it or lose it.

What does this have to do with offerings given to God through Churches and ministries?

What is put into the offering plate is actually the essence of someone's worship. God provides His property to individuals. It soaks for a while during which time it is prayed over. What is produced is an offering to God. This may be large or small, but it is the essence of that person's heart and worship to God. Just as the widow's mite in the Bible story.

The ministry is to treat this as precious essence and mix it with prayer and action in the right proportion to produce the best return for God. Each drop, or in this case dollar, is more than a dollar. It is the essence of heartfelt worship and prayer given to God for His ministry. Before it is used by the Church for any purpose, it should be prayed over and used in the most effective and beneficial way for God's purposes as He leads.

God will actually multiply the use of each dollar so treated.

If Churches and ministries actually viewed every dollar received in this way, ministry spending would change dramatically. No more travel by private jet, luxury cars, expensive programs or money wasted on unnecessary stuff.

The focus would be to share the Gospel, disciple the people to do the ministry, and help the needy of the community in the name of Jesus.

By way of example regarding this concept:

In a sermon delivered December 1, 1912 by Russell H. Conwell, pastor of what is now Temple Baptist Church, Pastor Conwell said the little girl's name was Hattie May Wiatt. He told her story. The story has been told and retold many times with some variations, and it can be found in all of its iterations on the internet. The following is the essence of the story.

A weeping young girl huddled in the rain on the curb near a small church. She had just been turned away and told that the church was just "too crowded" to let her in.

As the pastor of the church walked by he inquired as to why she was sitting in the rain and crying. She sobbed "I can't go to Sunday School".

Studying her shabby clothes and dirty appearance, the pastor knew the reason she had been excluded. Taking her by the hand he took her inside and found a place for her in the Sunday school class. The child was delighted that they found room for her. But, as she went to bed that night, she could not stop thinking of other children like her, who have no place to worship Jesus.

Two years later, this child lay dead from diphtheria, in one of the poor tenement buildings in the city. Her parents called for the pastor, who had befriended their daughter, to handle the final arrangements. As the little girl's body was being moved, a worn, dirty and crumpled red purse was found which seemed to have been rummaged from some trash heap. Inside was 57 cents and a note, scribbled in childish handwriting, which read: 'This is to help build the little church bigger so more children can go to Sunday school." For two years she had saved for this offering of love. When the pastor tearfully read that note, he knew instantly what he would do.

Carrying this note and the cracked, red pocketbook to the pulpit, he told the story of her unselfish love and devotion. He challenged his congregation to get busy and raise enough money for the larger building. The 57 pennies were exchanged for $250 of donations.

But the story does not end there.... A newspaper learned of the story and published it. It was read by a wealthy realtor who offered the church a parcel of land worth thousands. When told that the church could not pay so much, he sold it to the little church for 57 cents. (Some accounts of this story say the first payment was 57 cents, but that does not change the essence of the story).

Church members stepped up to the plate and made large donations and within a short time the little girl's gift had increased to $250,000.00 — a huge sum for the turn of the twentieth century. Her unselfish love, and gift of her essence of worship, had encouraged others.

When you are in the city of Philadelphia, look up Temple Baptist Church, with a seating capacity of 3,300. And be sure to visit Temple University, where thousands of students are educated.

Also check out the Good Samaritan Hospital and a Sunday school building which houses hundreds of beautiful children, built so that no child in the area will ever need to be left outside during Sunday school time.

In one of the rooms of this building hangs the picture of the little girl, Hattie May Wiatt, whose 57 cents, so sacrificially saved, made such remarkable history. Alongside of this picture is a portrait of her pastor, Dr. Russell H. Conwell.

This is a true story, which goes to demonstrate what God can do with the essence of someone's worship.

If Churches and ministries would pause to reflect on what each dollar given to them represented, they would never waste a drop of that essence. At times I want to weep when I see how God's money is misused by some Christian organizations.

When a person gives to the church, they are giving to God. Although giving involves checks, cash, credit cards, internet bank transfers, time and talent, it is first a transaction of the heart. When a gift is given to the church, it is cashed and recorded by the hands of people, and yet the gift is ultimately received by the hands of God.

Giving is both a spiritual transaction of the deepest and most personal nature between a person and their Provider, as well as a "ministry of giving" that meets the needs of others.

We not only need to be careful concerning how we handle and spend money, time and talent donated to the ministry; we need to be careful about how we solicit donations.

I wrote earlier about "prosperity theology" and the "legalistic tithe", both being unbiblical teachings. Now I am writing about how we should be teaching people about giving.

The leadership of Paul in the early church, especially to the Thessalonians and the Corinthians, provides some clear guidelines regarding how leaders are to teach stewardship.

- Paul taught principles and precepts of stewardship.

    "...we beg you to love them more and more. This should be your ambition: to live a quiet life, minding your own business and working with your hands, just as we commanded you before. As a result, people who are not Christians will respect the way you live, and you will not need to depend on others to meet your financial needs." 1 Thessalonians 4:10-12

    "Even while we were with you, we gave you this rule: 'Whoever does not work should not eat.' Yet we hear that some of you are living idle lives, refusing to work and wasting time meddling in other people's business. In the name of the Lord Jesus Christ, we appeal to such people-no, we command them: Settle down and get to work. Earn your own living." 2 Thessalonians 3:10-12

    "Don't team up with those who are unbelievers. How can goodness be a partner with wickedness? How can light live with darkness?" 2 Corinthians 6:14

    "But be sure that everything is done properly and in order." 1 Corinthians 14:40

    The teaching of Paul on the principles and precepts of stewardship is voluminous. I will stop with these few verses. You get the idea ... teach the principles.

- Paul modeled stewardship principles.

    "Paul lived and worked with them, for they were tentmakers just as he was." Acts 18:3

"For you know that you ought to follow our example. We were never lazy when we were with you. We never accepted food from anyone without paying for it. We worked hard day and night so that we would not be a burden to any of you. It wasn't that we didn't have the right to ask you to feed us, but we wanted to give you an example to follow." 2 Thessalonians 3:7-10

- Paul consistently reminded the believers of how the apostles modeled stewardship.

    "As apostles of Christ we certainly had a right to make some demands of you, but we were as gentle among you as a mother feeding and caring for her own children. We loved you so much that we gave you not only God's Good News but our own lives, too. Don't you remember, dear brothers and sisters, how hard we worked among you? Night and day we toiled to earn a living so that our expenses would not be a burden to anyone there as we preached God's Good News among you."
    1 Thessalonians 2:7-9

- Paul taught his listeners to be responsible for stewardship in their lives.

"This should be your ambition: to live a quiet life, minding your own business and working with your hands, just as we commanded you before.

As a result, people who are not Christians will respect the way you live, and you will not need to depend on others to meet your financial needs." 1 Thessalonians 4:11-12

- Paul taught in specifics about how to practice stewardship.

  "On every Lord's Day, each of you should put aside some amount of money in relation to what you have earned and save it for this offering. Don't wait until I get there and then try to collect it all at once."
  1 Corinthians 16:2

- Paul reinforced his teaching through his leadership team.

  "So we have urged Titus, who encouraged your giving in the first place, to return to you and encourage you to complete your share in this ministry of giving."
  2 Corinthians 8:6

- Paul gave examples through stories of faithfulness.

  "Now I want to tell you, dear brothers and sisters, what God in his kindness has done for the churches in Macedonia. Though they have been going through much trouble and hard times, their wonderful joy and deep poverty have overflowed in rich generosity.

  For I can testify that they gave not only what they could afford but far more. And they did it of their own free will. They begged us again and again for the gracious privilege of sharing in the gift for the Christians in Jerusalem.

  Best of all, they went beyond our highest hopes, for their first action was to dedicate themselves to the Lord and to us for whatever directions God might give them." 2 Corinthians 8:1-5

- Paul both encouraged and admonished his audience to excel in stewardship.

"Since you excel in so many ways — you have so much faith, such gifted speakers, such knowledge, such enthusiasm, and such love for us — now I want you to excel also in this gracious ministry of giving. I am not saying you must do it, even though the other churches are eager to do it.

This is one way to prove your love is real. You know how full of love and kindness our Lord Jesus Christ was. Though he was very rich, yet for your sakes he became poor, so that by his poverty he could make you rich.

I suggest that you finish what you started a year ago, for you were the first to propose this idea, and you were the first to begin doing something about it. Now you should carry this project through to completion just as enthusiastically as you began it. Give whatever you can according to what you have. If you are really eager to give, it isn't important how much you are able to give. God wants you to give what you have, not what you don't have. Of course, I don't mean you should give so much that you suffer from having too little.

I only mean that there should be some equality. Right now you have plenty and can help them. Then at some other time they can share with you when you need it. In this way, everyone's needs will be met. Do you remember what the Scriptures say about this? Those who gathered a lot had nothing left over, and those who gathered only a little had enough." 2 Corinthians 8:7-15

- Paul demonstrated transparency in his handling of gifts.

"I am thankful to God that he has given Titus the same enthusiasm for you that I have. He welcomed our request that he visit you again. In fact, he himself was eager to go and see you. We are also sending another brother with Titus. He is highly praised in all the churches as a preacher of the Good News.

He was appointed by the churches to accompany us as we take the offering to Jerusalem — a service that glorifies the Lord and shows our eagerness to help. By traveling together we will guard against any suspicion, for we are anxious that no one should find fault with the way we are handling this generous gift. We are careful to be honorable before the Lord, but we also want everyone else to know we are honorable.

And we are also sending with them another brother who has been thoroughly tested and has shown how earnest he is on many occasions. He is now even more enthusiastic because of his increased confidence in you. If anyone asks about Titus, say that he is my partner who works with me to help you. And these brothers are representatives of the churches. They are splendid examples of those who bring glory to Christ. So show them your love, and prove to all the churches that our boasting about you is justified." 2 Corinthians 8:16-24

"So I thought I should send these brothers ahead of me to make sure the gift you promised is ready. But I want it to be a willing gift, not one given under pressure." 2 Corinthians 9:5

- Paul followed up on commitments of giving.

"I really don't need to write to you about this gift for the Christians in Jerusalem. For I know how eager you are to help, and I have been boasting to our friends in Macedonia that you Christians in Greece were ready to send an offering a year ago.

In fact, it was your enthusiasm that stirred up many of them to begin helping. But I am sending these brothers just to be sure that you really are ready, as I told them you would be, with your money all collected. I don't want it to turn out that I was wrong in my boasting about you. I would be humiliated — and so would you — if some Macedonian Christians came with me, only to find that you still weren't ready after all I had told them!" 2 Corinthians 9:1-4

- Paul trained his leadership team.

"Tell those who are rich in this world not to be proud and not to trust in their money, which will soon be gone. But their trust should be in the living God, who richly gives us all we need for our enjoyment. Tell them to use their money to do good. They should be rich in good works and should give generously to those in need, always being ready to share with others whatever God has given them. By doing this they will be storing up their treasure as a good foundation for the future so that they may take hold of real life."
1 Timothy 6:17-19

- Paul silenced those who taught false doctrine in the church.

"For there are many insubordinate, both idle talkers and deceivers, especially those of the circumcision,

whose mouths must be stopped, who subvert whole households, teaching things which they ought not, for the sake of dishonest gain." Titus 1: 10 & 11

- Paul encouraged Christians to look for the return of Jesus.

"For if we believe that Jesus died and rose again, even so God will bring with Him those who sleep in Jesus. For this we say to you by the word of the Lord, that we who are alive and remain until the coming of the Lord will by no means precede those who are asleep. For the Lord Himself will descend from heaven with a shout, with the voice of an archangel, and with the trumpet of God, And the dead in Christ will rise first. Then we who are alive and remain shall be caught up together with them in the clouds to meet the Lord in the air, and thus we shall always be with the Lord."
I Thessalonians 4:14-17

There is no doubt that Paul's communication was intense; however, this was probably for a good reason. The Holy Spirit knew how difficult a topic this would be for spiritual leaders and givers. He wanted to reinforce the need and level of intensity for this type of communication. Paul expressed to his congregation the joy that comes from a life of giving as well as the obligation.

Please, do not deviate from God's Word when asking people to give and stick as closely as possible to the patterns presented in His Word.

This book has been written to every Christian who desires to follow Jesus and to know His purpose for their lives, but it is also written to Christian leaders. Those who teach and lead others.

Here are some suggested internal practices for church leaders about stewardship in the church.

Leadership

As the members of church families struggle with the spiritual battle surrounding money, it makes sense that the spiritual leader of the local church plays a significant role. The Senior Pastor should set the example in the area of stewardship by modeling a generous lifestyle. He should also set the example in stewardship education. He is the primary communicator of the church's vision. He needs to be actively involved in communicating the vision to the people that God has gifted to fulfill it; whether it is with financial resources or other areas of giftedness.

The important thing to note is that by empowering the Senior Pastor to play the key leadership role in encouraging generous giving and stewardship training, the church is not showing preference to large donors or financial matters. It is merely empowering the leader to provide the same level of spiritual leadership in the area of finances that we expect of him in other areas of ministry.

In 1 Timothy, Paul indicates that, among other things, those desiring to be overseers and deacons should be above reproach, a good manager of his own household and spiritually mature:

> *"It is a true saying that if someone wants to be an elder, he desires an honorable responsibility. For an elder must be a man whose life cannot be spoken against. He must be faithful to his wife. He must exhibit self-control, live wisely, and have a good reputation.*

He must enjoy having guests in his home and must be able to teach. He must not be a heavy drinker or be violent. He must be gentle, peace loving, and not one who loves money. He must manage his own family well, with children who respect and obey him. For if a man cannot manage his own household, how can he take care of God's church? An elder must not be a new Christian, because he might be proud of being chosen so soon, and the Devil will use that pride to make him fall. Also, people outside the church must speak well of him so that he will not fall into the Devil's trap and be disgraced." 1 Timothy 3:1-7

One characteristic of a spiritually mature person is faithfully seeking to be a good steward of all God provides, including giving to God from one's income and wealth.

The Bible describes the qualifications for leadership as well as the practices and convictions of a good steward. Through giving on a regular basis to the work of the church, a ministry leader lives the example of a committed member of the local church family and God's work through its body.

Therefore, all leaders of the church should be encouraged to pursue a lifestyle of Biblical stewardship and faithful financial support of the church.

With the desire of facilitating appropriate mutual accountability and encouragement for spiritual growth in this area, the following concepts should be discussed, on at least an annual basis as described below. This process is intended to be one of encouragement, as the Bible teaches in Hebrews 10:24-25, and is not to reflect an attitude of condemnation or pressure, as reflected in 2 Corinthians 9:7 and James 4:11-12.

Hebrews 10:24-25

"Think of ways to encourage one another to outbursts of love and good deeds. And let us not neglect our meeting together, as some people do, but encourage and warn each other, especially now that the day of his coming back again is drawing near."

2 Corinthians 9:7

"You must each make up your own mind as to how much you should give. Don't give reluctantly or in response to pressure. For God loves the person who gives cheerfully."

James 4:11-12

Don't speak evil against each other, my dear brothers and sisters. If you criticize each other and condemn each other, then you are criticizing and condemning God's law. But you are not a judge who can decide whether the law is right or wrong. Your job is to obey it. God alone, who made the law, can rightly judge among us. He alone has the power to save or to destroy. So what right do you have to condemn your neighbor?"

All Lay Leaders in key roles of leadership should be trained during the regular course of leadership development on Biblical stewardship, giving and support of their church.

Offering collection

Both the Old Testament and New Testament teach the tradition of bringing a gift to church as a regular act of worship. That said, the giving of gifts was not confined to take place solely at church, as believers are instructed to give directly to the poor, people in need or to those taking up collections to be dispersed abroad.

Recognizing these principles, providing a place and time in the weekend services for this important aspect of worship, is a vital part of giving biblically. The following are scriptural references relating to the act of bringing a gift to church as an act of worship.

The church provides a place to bring gifts.

> Mark 12:41-44
> *Jesus went over to the collection box in the Temple and sat and watched as the crowds dropped in their money. Many rich people put in large amounts. Then a poor widow came and dropped in two pennies. He called his disciples to him and said, "I assure you, this poor widow has given more than all the others have given. For they gave a tiny part of their surplus, but she, poor as she is, has given everything she has."*

Presenting an offering is a sacred moment between a person and God with significance greater than just a deposit of money, but in fact a moment for reflection, repentance, and connection with God.

> Matthew 5:23-24
> *"So if you are standing before the altar in the Temple, offering a sacrifice to God, and you suddenly remember that someone has something against you, leave your sacrifice there beside the altar. Go and be reconciled to that person. Then come and offer your sacrifice to God".*

There is significance to the timing of gifts. Here believers are instructed to set aside funds on every Lord's Day, an act of worship that takes place correlating with weekly worship.

1 Corinthians 16:2
"On every Lord's Day, each of you should put aside some amount of money in relation to what you have earned and save it for this offering. Don't wait until I get there and then try to collect it all at once."

Although believers are instructed to be private about our specific giving details to protect from pride, there is an importance and value to a public act of giving as others may be encouraged by people's generosity and faith.

2 Corinthians 9:2
"For I know how eager you are to help, and I have been boasting to our friends in Macedonia that you Christians in Greece were ready to send an offering a year ago. In fact, it was your enthusiasm that stirred up many of them to begin helping."

The mechanics of giving opportunities are orchestrated by the church, therefore we must be careful that this family worship opportunity is offered without pressure or embarrassment of any kind. Rather, we should create giving opportunities in such a way that people may experience great joy.

2 Corinthians 9:7
"You must each make up your own mind as to how much you should give. Don't give reluctantly or in response to pressure. For God loves the person who gives cheerfully."

You may be interested to know that at Mariners Church we did not pass the offering plate. This was the case so that no undo pressure was placed on the attendees.

There was a time of prayer during the service for the offering and occasional teaching about giving during this time.

The audience was told that receptacles were by every exit for the purpose of collecting an offering.

We estimated that over the course of each year this practice probably caused Mariners to forego about three million dollars in donations. But these potential donations would not have been contributed from the heart of the donor, but from the pressure of the plate passing. God does not want these donations and neither did Mariners Church. Plus, as I have demonstrated, God no doubt caused many more donations to go to Mariners that would not have otherwise been given, by virtue of how Mariners taught and modeled stewardship. Therefore, in the end, Mariners did not lose donations but gained donations. As you have read, God greatly blessed Mariners financially.

Trust God to speak to the hearts of His people through His Holy Spirit.

Finally, churches need to be above reproach in the way they collect, transport and process the offering, in order to protect the church, staff and volunteers from the occurrence of theft or false accusations of theft. This will be carried out by selecting trustworthy individuals who will keep the information confidential and by requiring two or more unrelated individuals (i.e. no blood relation, no close friends, no married couples, etc.) to be with the money at all times.

> 2 Corinthians 8:18-20
> *"We're sending a companion along with him, someone very popular in the churches for his preaching of the Message. But there's far more to him than popularity. He's rock-solid trustworthy. The churches handpicked him to go with us as we travel about doing this work of sharing God's gifts to honor God as well as we can, taking every precaution against scandal. We don't*

want anyone suspecting us of taking one penny of this money for ourselves."

The church should be committed to treat the entire process from the teaching of biblical giving to the deployment of gifts received as one of a sacred trust.

From the point of offering collections to final deployment, the church should be held to the highest level of accountability. Always be aware that interactions with givers take on a spiritual significance. Giving is a response of a worshipper's heart being prompted or encouraged toward generosity and faithful stewardship of God's provision in their lives.

Although the accounting department may handle the deposits of countless checks as does any secular organization, the nature of gifts given to the church reflects the deepest matters of a person's heart and holds eternal significance. It is their essence of worship.

Therefore, at all times during the journey of a gift as it leaves the hands of a giver to its ultimate destination, churches should treat the process and the people with the utmost respect.

Churches need to recognize and embrace that interactions with givers meet them at a powerful moment where a spiritual battle may be still in play. We strive to be grateful, professional, embrace the joy or even tension that may be a part of the moment, and yet we at all times remember this is not about us, but instead a transaction of a person's heart between them and their Provider.

Because giving is a powerful act of worship on behalf of a believer, it also comes with a significant spiritual battle. Giving is a transaction first of the heart where courageous, loving and humble decisions must be made in response to the Source of the blessings one has received. This is achieved by the alignment of one's heart with the love, faithfulness and generosity of God.

One of the surprising observations in the Luke passage about the two coins is that Jesus *"watched"*. What Jesus watched and saw was not as man sees, simply amounts of money deposited in a box.

What Jesus watched and saw was the condition of the giver's hearts. This story illustrates that it was the heart that was of Jesus' primary concern and that should be the primary concern of every church as well.

Therefore, be committed as a church to pray for the hearts of givers. Specifically, it should be a matter of course for the church leaders, as well as the lay team of Offering Counters that meets weekly to count offerings, to regularly pray for the hearts of the people in this area of giving.

Churches need to be committed to treat every dollar given into its care as if it were the widow's two pennies.

> 2 Corinthians 8:18-21
> *"We are also sending another brother with Titus. He is highly praised in all the churches as a preacher of the Good News. He was appointed by the churches to accompany us as we take the offering to Jerusalem - a service that glorifies the Lord and shows our eagerness to help. By traveling together we will guard against any suspicion, for we are anxious that no one should find fault with the way we are handling this generous gift. We are careful to be honorable before the Lord, but we also want everyone else to know we are honorable."*

Qualified professionals should be hired to account for the gifts in accordance with generally accepted accounting principles, and to prepare periodic reports of the gifts on a weekly, monthly, quarterly and annual basis, depending on the size of the church. These reports need to be reviewed by various oversight persons and committees.

In addition, an annual certified audit should be performed by an independent public accounting firm selected each year by the lay leadership. If a church is simply too small to afford such an annual audit, the financials should be reviewed by an independent qualified person or committee.

The annual budget

The annual budget is meant to be a strategic tool to allocate the financial resources of the church. The budgeting process provides a unique opportunity every year to align the initiatives and plans of the church with the allocation of financial resources. More importantly, the annual budgeting process is a spiritual journey whereby we hear God's voice (through prayer) and follow Him.

The first step in the budgeting process is to anticipate the giving/income. For the operating budget prayerfully consider and establish the general offering percentage increase the team believes that God will provide for the year ahead. When identifying this percentage, it is important to hold at the forefront the desire to be good stewards and to base the forecast on historical trends, changes within the congregation and general economic forecasts while stepping out in faith and being dependent on God to provide.

Once this amount is identified, it determines the maximum expenditures for the church operations and ministries.

The second step is to allocate the expenses, in order to be good stewards of the dollars anticipated to be received by the church. The church should be committed to treat every dollar given into its care as if it were the essence of someone's worship. It is with this mindset that the expense budgets are created.

It is also important that each ministry's budget reflects, and is supported by the current year's operation. Expenses may be equal to or lower than projected revenue, never in excess of projected revenue, unless a reserve was established for this purpose. It is not a requirement to budget expenses for all the projected income. There may be years where a portion of the expense budget is left unallocated.

Church debt

In the life of a growing church, the question arises of whether or not the church should incur debt. This is an important issue that deserves careful consideration and prayer because there are no examples in scripture of using debt for any building programs or ministry purposes.

On one hand, it may seem completely unrealistic to assume that a major building project could be accomplished in today's day and age without the use of debt. On the other hand, there are many examples of churches that have suffered the consequences of going deeply into debt over ill-advised building projects or expansion plans.

One church may be held back in its growth because of a "no debt" policy while another may be saddled with debt by over-extending itself.

The considerations of using debt may boil down to issues such as timing, scope and giving potential. "Is it feasible to build within the time frame and at the level we believe God desires?"

"Will God provide and will our people give enough money to fully fund the need in advance?"

These issues create the dilemma of debt. If the total funds required to achieve the vision is believed to exceed the present giving potential of the church, debt may become a viable option as long as it conforms to the values and guidelines contained herein.

Scripture does not prohibit debt, but rather, warns of its dangers and discourages its use as a general principle:

> Proverbs 22:7
> *"Just as the rich rule the poor, so the borrower is servant to the lender."*

> Romans 13:8
> *"Let no debt remain outstanding, except the continuing debt to love one another, for he who loves his fellowman has fulfilled the law."*

Although Scripture does not prohibit debt nor refer to indebtedness as a sinful act, the Bible does teach that a heart's motivation to incur debt may be sinful in origin. The following scriptures highlight two traps that can lead to sinful motivations: The trap of presuming upon the future and the trap of wanting to get rich quickly.

> James 4:13-15
> *"Look here, you people who say, "Today or tomorrow we are going to a certain town and will stay there a year. We will do business there and make a profit." How do you know what will happen tomorrow? For your life is like the morning fog — it's here a little while, then it's gone. What you ought to say is, "If the Lord wants us to, we will live and do this or that."*

Proverbs 28:20
"The trustworthy will get a rich reward. But the person who wants to get rich quick will only get into trouble."

Proverbs 28:22
"A greedy person tries to get rich quick, but it only leads to poverty."

Proverbs 13:11
"Wealth from get-rich-quick schemes quickly disappears; wealth from hard work grows."

It is for these reasons that careful consideration and prayer need to be given to any decision to incur debt. Whenever human hearts are involved, it is possible for a church (especially after a history of great provision) to get ahead of God, become overconfident and presume upon a future that is not part of His plan. It is also possible to get ahead of God and desire to "get rich quick" by expanding ministry or facilities sooner than God's time frame may call for.

A number of examples exist in the Bible where leaders communicated needs and people responded by giving. In some instances, *more was given than needed* as with Moses and the Tabernacle:

Exodus 36:5-7
"We have more than enough materials on hand now to complete the job the LORD has given us to do," they exclaimed. So Moses gave the command, and this message was sent throughout the camp:

"Bring no more materials! You have already given more than enough." So the people stopped bringing their offerings. Their contributions were more than enough to complete the whole project."

Philippians 4:18
"At the moment I have all I need — more than I need! I am generously supplied with the gifts you sent me with Epaphroditus. They are a sweet-smelling sacrifice that is acceptable to God and pleases him."

Other times, less was given than was needed. God allowed the consequences of shortfall, hardship and diminished ministry opportunity:

Nehemiah 13:10-12
"I also discovered that the Levites had not been given what was due them, so they and the singers who were to conduct the worship services had all returned to work their fields. I immediately confronted the leaders and demanded, "Why has the Temple of God been neglected?" Then I called all the Levites back again and restored them to their proper duties. And once more all the people of Judah began bringing their tithes of grain, new wine and olive oil to the Temple storerooms."

Malachi 3:8-10
"Should people cheat God? Yet you have cheated me! But you ask, 'What do you mean? When did we ever cheat you?' You have cheated me of the tithes and offerings due to me. You are under a curse, for your whole nation has been cheating me.

Bring all the tithes into the storehouse so there will be enough food in my Temple. If you do,' says the LORD Almighty, 'I will open the windows of heaven for you.

I will pour out a blessing so great you won't have enough room to take it in! Try it! Let me prove it to you!"

And then other cases where the ultimate amount available for ministry purposes was left to be determined by the response of people's hearts and the amount of their giving decisions.

2 Corinthians 9:7
"You must each make up your own mind as to how much you should give. Don't give reluctantly or in response to pressure. For God loves the person who gives cheerfully."

2 Corinthians 8:12
"If you are really eager to give, it isn't important how much you are able to give. God wants you to give what you have, not what you don't have."

Scripture mentions three major "building programs": the Tabernacle, the Temple and the rebuilding of the Temple. Each occurs in the Old Testament and was financed by upfront giving without the use of debt of any kind. Givers comprised a faithful group of believers who would seek God's direction and give sacrificially what they were able to give.

In all three "fund raising" situations, we see the power of the Holy Spirit moving upon people's hearts directing them to give or release the resources required.

In the building of The Tabernacle (*Exodus 35, 36*), we see God powerfully moving on the hearts of people to fulfill the funding requirements. Giving is described as: "willing heart," "whose heart stirred him," "whose heart moved him," and "everyone who could."

The same was true in building the Temple. Three times in a single passage it says that the people "offered willingly" (*1 Chronicles 29: 6, 9, 17*).

And hundreds of years later in the rebuilding of The Temple (*Ezra 1, 2, 7*), "everyone whose heart God had moved," "gave freewill offerings," "according to their ability they gave." The singular focus for their source of funding ministry was always the current gifts of believers prompted by the heart of God.

There is no place in scripture that reflects either: 1) An initial plan for a ministry objective that included both a debt and cash component; or 2) a subsequent "plan B" where a giving shortfall was later subsidized by the use of debt.

It is noteworthy to consider David's prayer of thanksgiving after God fully supplied their needs for the Temple. There is an overwhelming moment of celebration as the entire financial need for the building of the Temple was met in advance through the gifts of the people.

All their thanksgiving and praise went to God alone for His gracious provision! Consider how their feelings may have been different if David and the people were dealing with only half the resources given currently and carrying half of the required amount as debt on the books for years to come.

> 1 Chronicles 29: 9-14
> *"The people rejoiced over the offerings, for they had given freely and wholeheartedly to the LORD, and King David was filled with joy. Then David praised the LORD in the presence of the whole assembly: "O LORD, the God of our ancestor Israel, may you be praised forever and ever!*

Yours, O Lord, is the greatness, the power, the glory, the victory, and the majesty. Everything in the heavens and on earth is yours, O Lord, and this is your kingdom. We adore you as the one who is over all things. Riches and honor come from you alone, for you rule over everything. Power and might are in your hand, and it is at your discretion that people are made great and given strength. O our God, we thank you and praise your glorious name! But who am I, and who are my people, that we could give anything to you? Everything we have has come from you, and we give you only what you have already given us!"

In each of these three Old Testament fund raising/building campaigns, the work was not started until it was fully funded and it was obvious the project could be completed without borrowing.

In the New Testament there are no examples of a building project for a church. All examples of fundraising, (e.g.: *Acts 4*, Early church; *2 Corinthians 8 & 9*, Poor Christians in Jerusalem), are funded on a current basis as people gave willingly to a ministry need. There are no indications of funding ever being supplemented with any form of debt.

Jesus (speaking of the cost of following Him) uses a practical illustration about a building project commenced without thoughtful planning and the assurance of enough money to carry it through to completion.

Luke 14:28-31
"But don't begin until you count the cost. For who would begin construction of a building without first getting estimates and then checking to see if there is enough money to pay the bills?

Otherwise, you might complete only the foundation before running out of funds. And then how everyone would laugh at you! They would say, 'There's the person who started that building and ran out of money before it was finished!' Or what king would ever dream of going to war without first sitting down with his counselors and discussing whether his army of ten thousand is strong enough to defeat the twenty thousand soldiers who are marching against him?"

So that brings us to the question of whether using debt today in our 21st century church context is appropriate. There are substantial competing tensions surrounding this issue today: the high price of land and buildings, the ability to use and manage debt to accelerate and leverage ministry impact, less than optimal giving levels in the church due to lack of maturity or obedience, and not the least of which is the seemingly impossible prospect of building out the church in the scope of which we believe to be our calling without the use of debt.

These issues are not easily answered by simply observing that times are different today, considering the relative poverty that was the context of the Old Testament building projects.

Before we establish some guiding values, let's review some additional scriptural principles regarding indebtedness:

Indebtedness creates a servitude to others in addition to God:

> Proverbs 22:7*"Just as the rich rule the poor, so the borrower is servant to the lender."*

God holds all we need and God creates the liquidity to bless our work in His proper time.

Deuteronomy 28:12a
"The LORD will send rain at the proper time from his rich treasury in the heavens to bless all the work you do"...

God used indebtedness as a curse for Israel and being debt free as a blessing.

Deuteronomy 28:12b
..."You will lend to many nations, but you will never need to borrow from them."

Deuteronomy 28:44-45
"They will lend money to you, not you to them. They will be the head, and you will be the tail! If you refuse to listen to the LORD your God and to obey the commands and laws he has given you, all these curses will pursue and overtake you until you are destroyed."

Indebtedness is to be a temporary condition with the debtor intent upon "finishing repayment" and be debt free.

Romans 13:8
"Pay all your debts, except the debt of love for others. You can never finish paying that! If you love your neighbor, you will fulfill all the requirements of God's law."

Deuteronomy 15:1
"At the end of every seventh year you must cancel your debts."

No one would argue the ideal of desiring to fully fund all ministry initiatives in advance without the use of debt. We are drawn in and compelled by what God did with His chosen people Israel as they responded to the Spirit and gave generously to fully meet the need. We believe God can do the same today, and in fact He has done this with many churches.

So with confidence in God's ability to provide at any level He desires, the church should seek to understand God's unique plan to hear His voice and follow Him.

The question is, "Would God lead or permit a church to utilize a prudent amount of debt to accomplish His plans?"

From my review of scripture, I see the optimal scenario with Israel; no debt, buildings built and great celebration for God's provision on a current basis. Scripture warns about the dangers of indebtedness and the vulnerability that comes with it, but stops short of prohibiting the use of debt.

In the reality of today's economy, many faithful stewards have engaged a component of debt for purposes such as housing, ministry or church facilities. As biblical wisdom and prudent financial planning principles are applied along with the conviction of disciplined debt retirement and ultimately debt freedom, many have observed God's blessings in their plans as well.

Experience would tell us, that as we consider how the Holy Spirit works in our own personal lives, and in many churches before us, the use of debt may somehow fall into a category of a "grace" that can be a part of a God-honoring plan.

That under certain circumstances, though not quite favorable, with prayerful consideration and wise planning, God will at times allow a person, family or church to engage a component of debt to be used as a tool to accomplish important purposes such as shelter or facilities.

As biblical wisdom and values are applied along with the conviction of disciplined debt retirement and ultimately debt freedom, one can observe God blessing such plans as well.

Again to reiterate, the decision to utilize debt is of great seriousness. Many individuals and churches have made a decision to take on debt at a point in time only to suffer harsh consequences for many years to come.

The answer to God's plan for your church will not be found by following personal desires, natural wisdom, what other churches have done, or by following the recommendations of professional consultants. Churches must diligently and prayerfully seek God's direction.

> James 1:5
> *"If you need wisdom — if you want to know what God wants you to do — ask him, and he will gladly tell you. He will not resent you asking."*

> Proverbs 15:22
> *"Plans go wrong for lack of advice; many counselors bring success."*

> Proverbs 16:3
> *"Commit your work to the Lord, and then your plans will succeed."*

> Luke 14:28-30
> *"But don't begin until you count the cost. For who would begin construction of a building without first getting estimates and then checking to see if there is enough money to pay the bills? Otherwise, you might complete only the foundation before running out of funds.*

And then how everyone would laugh at you! They would say, "There's the person who started that building and ran out of money before it was finished!"

Finally, the church is a living example for what is taught to the congregation. The message should always be for people to avoid the "bondage" of debt and pursue the goal of a debt-free lifestyle.

There are many scriptures related to debt and building projects, however, none of them specifically prohibit debt. The church should seek God's will through prayer before making a decision to incur debt. If a decision is made to incur debt, prayerfully establish the following principles, or guidelines, in order to protect the church from incurring too much debt:

1. Upon the completion of the project, the church's intention should be to become debt free. There should be a plan to accomplish this.

2. All decisions for debt should ultimately be made at the governing level according to the church guidelines.

3. The overall budget impact, to meet the debt service requirements, should not encumber the church's ability to perform ministry.

4. Before a church incurs capital campaign related debt, there should be a clear, compelling vision for the related project. The indication that such a vision exists is the level of financial commitment and giving directed to the project by the congregation. If a church begins the process pre-disposed toward debt, it may limit the amount people will give. People may not rise to the level of commitment God desires if there is a sense the project is covered or hedged through debt.

5. After the impact on ministries is satisfactorily considered, future debt service requirements should be reviewed to ensure debt service does not exceed 20% of the general operating budget. If debt is being incurred for a building project, this calculation should be based on conservatively projected revenues at the completion of the project or applicable phase of construction. The calculation should include only those revenues that are available for debt service and should exclude revenues for designated funds (i.e. Outreach). The debt service calculation should be based on a 20 year amortization and expected market interest rates.

In conclusion, it is best to avoid debt, but if debt must be incurred it should be in a conservative amount in relation to the church's anticipated revenue. I must point out that at Mariners Church I arranged for the church to borrow twenty-five percent of the cost of the campus build-out. This debt was however repaid very quickly, and by immediately commencing the project, Mariners saved considerable amounts of money on the cost of materials which thereafter increased rapidly.

Teach stewardship

Jesus' ministry and the work of the church are devoted to the redemption and transformation of people's spiritual hearts.

> *John 8:31-32*
> *Jesus said to the people who believed in him, "You are truly my disciples if you keep obeying my teachings. And you will know the truth, and the truth will set you free."*

The primary objectives of stewardship ministry are to educate people according to the Bible's teaching regarding biblical stewardship principles and provide personal encouragement for people to live passionately with a steward's heart.

In order to reach the breadth of the congregation, educational components should be reflected in the weekend services as well as all appropriate life stage and affinity group ministries.

The message of the ministry is to be directed to the full spectrum of believers in the congregation, from those who are unaware of the basic concepts or practices of biblical stewardship to the mature believer being encouraged to passionately pursue the full expression of their steward's heart.

Since "felt needs" are often a gateway to ministering to people's hearts, various practical financial education vehicles should be offered including basic budgeting, financial planning and estate planning.

Provide avenues of giving for everyone. There is no poverty in Newport Beach, California where Mariners Church is primarily located. Therefore to give to the poor in the community Mariners adopted a neighborhood in the closest impoverished community.

Mariners Church gave assistance with money, food, clothing, and housing, opened a thrift store, taught the children, and shared the gospel. Most new givers at Mariners began by giving of their time, talent and treasure to this ministry which was named Lighthouse Ministry.

Whenever there was a disaster anywhere in the world, Mariners Church was there with assistance, both monetary and labor. Our people responded in overwhelming ways thanks to the ministry and leadership of Pastor Gene Molway.

God alone knows the heart of the giver. The giver should ensure his motives are pure. Is he giving to show his love, trust and obedience in God? It is the responsibility of the leadership and ministries of every church to ensure that all teaching and requests for giving are completed in ways that encourage pure obedience.

At Mariners Church, Pastor Kenton Beshore instituted an eight week course in basic Christianity, to be taught to every attendee of Mariners. One week was fully devoted to teaching Biblical stewardship. This program was call "Rooted", and the curriculum may be obtained by contacting Mariners Church.

Other words that describe a proper attitude regarding money and giving are:

Cheerful – God loves a cheerful giver. *II Corinthians 9:7*

Honesty – Be honest with money in thoughts and deeds. *Proverbs 28:6*

Humility – Do not be egotistical. *Romans 12:16-17*

Forgiveness – Forgive the debts and wrongs of others. *Matthew 18:23-35*

Thankfulness – Always show an attitude of gratefulness. *I Thessalonians 5:18*

Obedience – Be doers of God's Word. *James 1:22*

Contentment – Be satisfied with what God provides. *Philippians 4:11*

Trust – Place your confidence in God. *Luke 12:29-31*

The church should clearly teach that deeds of righteousness must not be done for self-glorification. God clearly instructs us to give to an audience of one and, as a church; we should not take any action contrary to the intent of God's direction to the individual members of our church body:

Matthew 6:1-4

Take care! Don't do your good deeds publicly, to be admired, because then you will lose the reward from your Father in heaven. When you give a gift to someone in need, don't shout about it as the hypocrites do – blowing trumpets in the synagogues and streets to call attention to their acts of charity! I assure you, they have received all the reward they will ever get. But when you give to someone, don't tell your left hand what your right hand is doing. Give your gifts in secret, and your Father, who knows all secrets, will reward you.

The intentions and instructions in *Matthew 6* are directed at the giver and not the church; however, the church should be cautious that none of our actions contribute to a donor developing a prideful approach to giving.

When we surrender every area of our lives– including our finances–to God, then we are free to trust Him to meet our needs. But if we would rather hold tightly to those things that we possess, then we find ourselves in bondage to those very things. – Larry Burkett

CONCLUSION

In light of all that I've just written concerning God's principles of stewardship and His supporting precepts, it is important that I conclude with a basic fact.

The Christian life can never be explained in terms of me, or my actions. I, in my efforts, can seek to follow God's precepts and therefore attempt to reflect His principles, but if this is done of my own motivation and effort, then it is of no effect spiritually.

For example, if I choose to donate one million dollars to XYZ Christian University, and I do it so that the University will honor, or in some way recognize me (i.e. my name on a building or my receiving an honorary PhD), this gift may achieve my end, but my imitating the precept "giving" will be a sin in my life, and not Godly stewardship. Godliness is the exclusive result of God's work in me and can never be the result of my imitating God for my own purposes. Again - Godliness is God reproducing Himself in me!

Major W. Ian Thomas in his book *The Mystery of Godliness* presents a great illustration:

"No man has seen electricity at any time, yet an electric light bulb is so designed that whenever it receives the invisible current, expression is given to the invisible in terms of light.

It would not be true to say that the bulb is giving light, for it has no power to do so apart from the current which it receives: its behavior as a "light-giver" is the direct and exclusive consequence of the activity of the electricity in it and through it. The current is the cause, light is the effect, and though you can see the effect, you still cannot see the cause, though both represent the same source of energy!

You can enjoy the light, but you still cannot say that you have seen electricity! You can only say that you have seen a pure expression of it. In the same way, your behavior was intended by God to be a pure expression of His divine nature, though He remains unseen, and you can no more produce this effect of yourself, than a bulb can produce light of itself! Try and you will soon be exhausted, and at best you will only produce a shabby imitation of the real thing. It may impress you, but it certainly will not impress anyone else!" [xxii]

Once I accept that God alone can make me Godly, only then am I free to know God and allow Him to establish His image in me. God is not reliant upon me trying to conform to certain patterns of behavior or following certain rules. God alone will produce the behavior or fruit in me.

> *"You have died with Christ, and he has set you free from the evil powers of this world. So why do you keep on following rules of the world, such as, 'Don't handle, don't eat, don't touch.' Such rules are mere human teaching about things that are gone as soon as we use them. These rules may seem wise because they require strong devotion, humility, and severe bodily discipline. But they have no effect when it comes to conquering a person's evil thoughts and desires."* Colossians 2:20-23

God created man so that man would be in the "image" of God while God remained unseen. In other words, God flowing in and through man could produce an effect - God-likeness or Godliness.

> *"The Son reflects God's own glory, and everything about him represents God exactly. He sustains the universe by the mighty power of his command. After he died to cleanse us from the stain of sin, he sat down in the place of honor at the right hand of the majestic God of heaven."* Hebrews 1:3

Godliness deals with the motives of a person, and not with the outward deeds or appearances. Godliness is having God's moral character - Holiness, Love, Truthfulness, Mercy, Faithfulness, Goodness, Patience and Justice.

Unlike stewardship, which God gave as man's vocation in life, the principles that mirror God's moral character have no precepts, or rules of moral conduct for us to follow. This fruit is produced by God alone, not through our own effort. What we have is evidence of the principle in the believer's life.

We heard from Dr. Oscar Thompson earlier. Now another word from his book, _Concentric Circles of Concern_.

I have a beautiful martin house on a little hill out in my backyard. It is for purple martins, birds who eat their weight in mosquitoes and other pesky insects each day. It is on a telescoping pole. Several months ago when I was out of town, one of the nuts on the pole slipped; the martin house dropped down. When I got back home, I found it about four feet off the ground.

Now, the martins did not seem bothered too much, but I was afraid the cats would get to them. So I went out to raise it. Of course, I was staring the birds right in the face. They scattered like a covey of quail and really fussed at me. I ran the pole all the way up and secured it.

But one old bird in that group decided I had done something terribly wrong. Now every time I walk out into the backyard, she flies to about sixty feet and dives at me, coming about twelve inches from my head. Then, just as she passes my head, she goes "chirrup!" She does not bother Damaris (my daughter); she does not bother our puppies, Burfaldine or Neigette; she does not bother Carolyn (my wife); she does not bother our guests. Just me!

I was standing out in the backyard several days later when I said to her, "You dummy, don't you know I was lifting your house back up so a cat, skunk, or whatever could not bother your babies?" But she, like some fighter plane coming out of a cloud, just dived down and buzzed right over my head.

I said, "I wish I could communicate with you, but I cannot. I do not know bird language." I tried it. I went "chirrup," but she just kept coming back.

Do you see the point? God said, "I want to communicate with people." Jesus Christ entered history. John 1:14 says that Jesus is the Word. God sent Jesus to build a bridge to people, to be able to communicate with them, to be able to develop a relationship with them. Jesus is the One who reveals the character of the Father. Isn't that beautiful? Jesus built the bridge between God and people so that we can have a relationship with God.

Bearing fruit is the nature of Jesus. I once heard someone ask a black man, "What is a Christian?"

He smiled and replied, "Just Jesus running around in a black body." Or a white one, or a red one, or a yellow one, or whatever else.

Bearing fruit is Jesus Christ manifesting his character in our lives, Jesus' life-style in us. Listen carefully. Jesus wants his lifestyle to be manifested in your life."

Remember, Paul said that God has given to us two things: the Word of reconciliation and the ministry of reconciliation (2 Cor. 5:18-19). Our lives are to be linked with God since God by his grace and by the cross linked us with himself. Then he gives us that ability to reach out and build bridges to a lost world. That is what life is all about. This is bearing fruit.

When your life is bearing his fruit, you are bearing his life. You do not produce the fruit, he does. You bear it.

Jesus said, "I am the vine, you are the branches"; (John 15:5). In other words, you are a glorified grape rack. All you can do is bear the fruit. You cannot produce it. The vine, which is Jesus, produces it. Have you ever seen a tree saying, "Oh, I just have to produce some fruit"? No. It just does what it is designed to do."[xxiii]

Thanks Doc., for that message. See you soon.

My wife Suzanne and I went on a short three day cruise to Mexico several years ago. While shopping in Ensenada, we saw a lot of Gucci, Rolex, and other fine watches for very cheap prices.

Cartier makes a watch called a "Benior" that retailed in California, and most other places at that time, for around $20,000. We could have purchased this watch in Mexico for about $20. Well, we could have purchased a copy of this watch in Mexico for about $20.

Every Cartier watch has certain outward evidences that it is a genuine Cartier watch. The name Cartier stamped into the watch is one such evidence.

These Cartier copies in Ensenada had all the outward appearances, or evidences that they were genuine. I'm sure that an experienced jeweler could look on the inside of the watch and determine that it was not genuine. And if one were to wear such a watch for a period of time, I'm quite certain that it would show signs of not being genuine. The wrist turns green, it stops running, etc. The inside would just not have the same quality as the original it purports to copy.

Also, no matter how hard the maker of the imposter watch tried, he could not make a genuine Cartier Benior watch. Why? It is genuine only if manufactured by the Cartier Company.

So, every genuine Cartier watch has the name Cartier stamped into the watch, but every watch with the name Cartier stamped into it is not genuine. You must look on the inside to determine its authenticity. Outward evidences can be deceiving.

We are each a mystery, understood only by God.

Now we humans have a way of deceiving others and we can even deceive ourselves as James says. There are counterfeit Christians.

How do counterfeit Christians convince others and themselves to believe they are genuine Christians and on the narrow path when in fact they are on the wide path which leads to death?

Let me suggest four possible ways. There are probably many ways.

1. Like the fake Cartier watches, people put on the outward appearances of being born again believers. They observe what other Christians do and then do the same things. They go to Church, teach Sunday school or tithe.

You cannot make yourself a child of God by doing things that a child of God does, any more than you could make yourself an heir to the Queen of England by walking around in royal clothes and waving kindly at people. You have to have been born into the royal family. But appearances will fool people and soon you may believe it yourself.

2. They tell their story not God's story. What they did as opposed to what God did. Just like those that Jesus talked about in the Matthew seven passage. "Have we not done things in your name?"

3. They have knowledge of God thru hearsay. Knowledge by hearsay is counterfeit knowledge, made up only of things others have told us about God. Such knowledge might come through years of listening to sermons at Church, on the radio or T.V., and reading good Christian books by good Christian authors. These things can be beneficial, but they can also become a substitute for personally walking with God. We end up only knowing Him thru hearsay.

4. They are textualists. What is a textualist? A.W. Tozer, a Pastor who died in 1963 but not before he wrote the book "The Pursuit of God", describes the textualist as a person who assumes that because he or she affirms the Bible's veracity, they automatically possesses the things of which the Bible speaks.

For example, if one agrees with the biblical definition of faith, found in Hebrews 11, then a textualist will assume that they already possess such faith, even if all their choices in life prove otherwise. If they agree with Paul's words, then they are sure they possess the reality of Paul's words. If they accept every word of Paul as inspired, then every experience that Paul describes in the Christian life must already be theirs. In other words, the textualist lives as if affirming the words of the Bible is equivalent to having their reality in their own life.

Of all times throughout history now is not the time for self-deception or the counterfeit Christian life. The King is coming!

And He is coming very soon, but He is coming only for the true believer. The one on the narrow path going toward the narrow gate.

Make very sure you are on the right path. Your eternity depends on it.

Give cheerfully, regularly, and sacrificially - live out your life as God's steward. God will direct you and He will bestow eternal blessings as he looks into your heart and discerns your motives. Outward appearances are meaningless.

> "The Pharisees, who dearly loved their money, heard all this and scoffed at him. Then he said to them, 'You like to appear righteous in public, but God knows your hearts. What this world honors is detestable in the sight of God." Luke 16:14-15

We looked at the life of John Wesley earlier. He spoke often and accurately about stewardship after his conversion. In one of his sermons he summed it up thusly: "Earn all you can." "Save all you can." "Give all you can."

Our attitude toward money, wealth, generosity and giving are some of the most frequently discussed topics in Scripture. God knows our attitude regarding money can be a barrier in our relationship with Him:

> "But people who long to be rich fall into temptation and are trapped by many foolish and harmful desires that plunge them into ruin and destruction. For the love of money is at the root of all kinds of evil. And some people, craving money, have wandered from the faith and pierced themselves with many sorrows."
> 1 Timothy 6:9-10

God desires an intimate relationship with us. He wants us to experience the abundance He has to offer when we trust Him and place Him first in our lives. However, we live in a world which values and honors those who have financial riches and encourages us to hoard and increase our financial net worth.

The world demands that we focus on monetary issues and attempt to solve them ourselves rather than trusting God for the fulfillment of our daily needs. This kind of attitude results in financial bondage. As we have seen, God is most concerned with the focus of our hearts.

God has been consistent since the beginning of time regarding our offerings to Him. They are to be voluntary, cheerful, proportional, regular, sacrificial and generous.

God is more interested in our submissive hearts to give than he is in sacrificial acts. It is the obedience of our hearts that changes our lives and honors God.

But Samuel replied, "What is more pleasing to the LORD: your burnt offerings and sacrifices or your obedience to his voice? Listen! Obedience is better than sacrifice, and submission is better than offering the fat of rams." 1 Samuel 15:22

At the outset of this book I told the story of Mariners Church. Well, I told part of the story. I am sure that the Mariners' narrative is continuing to unfold, but at the time I was there, a change of heart swept over the congregation of Mariners. People grasp hold of the reality that they were created for a purpose … to be God's Steward!

This heart change is reflected in one of the letters I received after Mariners implemented Biblical stewardship teaching. This letter is similar to the many such responses received.

When the white paper on stewardship was submitted to the Mariners Church Elder Board, Mark Thomas was the Chairman of that board. After he reviewed the white paper he and his family prayed about the message contained in that paper, and Mark wrote a lengthy letter concerning his family's journey. With Mark's permission, part of that letter is below.

Mark is a fellow CPA, a financial expert and a Senior Partner with the premier CPA firm in the world. He is also a devoted follower of Jesus Christ. He and his family came to really understand the message of being God's Steward.

An excerpt from Mark's letter:

"We are on a journey. Our hearts' desire is to know God's Word and courageously follow it. We don't want to settle for anything less than radical abandonment to Him.

> But since you excel in everything — in faith, in speech, in knowledge, in complete earnestness and in the love we have kindled in you — see that you also excel in this grace of giving. (2 Corinthians 8:7)

Re-Setting Our Perspective: It is all His!

Sacrifice includes the recognition of what we are giving is an investment in eternity. The current sacrifice of giving pales in comparison to the eternal reward – making short-term sacrifices to gain long-term rewards. We must remember that Heaven, not earth, is our home. Martin Luther said, "I have held many things in my hands and lost them all. But whatever I have placed in God's hands that I still possess."

What does it Look Like to be Radically Abandoned to God?

> He sent them out to proclaim the kingdom of God and to heal the sick. ³ He told them: "Take nothing for the journey — no staff, no bag, no bread, no money, no extra shirt. (Luke 9:2)

> As they were walking along the road, a man said to him, "I will follow you wherever you go." Jesus replied, "Foxes have dens and birds have nests, but the Son of Man has no place to lay his head."

He said to another man, "Follow me." But he replied, "Lord, first let me go and bury my father." Jesus said to him, "Let the dead bury their own dead, but you go and proclaim the kingdom of God." Still another said, "I will follow you, Lord; but first let me go back and say goodbye to my family." Jesus replied, "No one who puts a hand to the plow and looks back is fit for service in the kingdom of God. (Luke 9:57-62)

We are tempted to replace what is radical about our faith with what is comfortable. Jesus tells these prospective followers to abandon everything – their needs, their desires, even their family.

If anyone comes to me and does not hate father and mother, wife and children, brothers and sisters – yes, even their own life – such a person cannot be my disciple. (Luke 14:26)
In the same way, those of you who do not give up everything you have cannot be my disciples. (Luke 14:33)

We are to reorient our entire lives around Him. Our plans and dreams are to be swallowed up in His.

As Jesus started on his way, a man ran up to him and fell on his knees before him. "Good teacher," he asked, "what must I do to inherit eternal life?" "Why do you call me good?" Jesus answered. "No one is good – except God alone. You know the commandments: 'You shall not murder, you shall not commit adultery, you shall not steal, you shall not give false testimony, you shall not defraud, honor your father and mother.'"

"Teacher," he declared, "all these I have kept since I was a boy." Jesus looked at him and loved him. "One thing you lack," he said. "Go, sell everything you have and give to the poor, and you will have treasure in heaven. Then come, follow me." (Mark 10:17-21)

The dangerous reality is that we have to give up everything to follow Jesus. This is a call to leave certainty for uncertainty, safety for danger, self-preservation for self-denunciation. It is entirely possible that He may tell us to sell everything we have and give it to the poor, in exchange for treasures in heaven. We are called to abandon the attachments of this world. In the end, we are not giving anything away at all. We have found something worth losing everything else for."

Just as so many did at Mariners Church, Mark Thomas read the white paper, prayed about the Biblically-based message it contained, and believed what he read. The white paper, like this book, was filled with God's Word.

Pete Ochs was at Mariners Church when the white paper was written, and he has since written a book entitled _"A High Impact Life ... Love Your Purpose, Live With Passion, Leverage Your Platform"_. An excerpt:

"For the first time in my life I began to ask those uncomfortable, penetrating questions. What's my purpose? What am I passionate about? What's my calling? And that all-encompassing question: Why do I exist? ...All this led me to one clear and unequivocal conclusion – my purpose in life was not to live for myself but to live for something greater. That simple commitment changed my life. I told God that from that day forward I would strive to live like a steward and not an owner. Everything I had would be considered His and I would steward it as faithfully as I could."xxiv

It does seem that the Scripture-based message contained in that Mariners Church white paper continues to produce ripples of impact, even far beyond Mariners Church.

You have now read the message of your purpose, to be God's Steward, as told from Scripture - Genesis thru Revelation.

What will it mean for your life?

END NOTES

[i] Anonymous

[ii] D. James Kennedy, Evangelism Explosion, Tyndale House Publishers, 1997, page 38.

[iii] W. Oscar Thompson, Concentric Circles of Concern, Broadman & Holman Publishers, 1999, pages 19 – 20.

[iv] A. w. Tozer, The Knowledge of the Holy, Harper Collins Publishers, 1961, page 16

[v] Stanley Tam, God Owns My Business, Christian Publications, Inc., 1969, preface
[vi] Ibid, page 54
[vii] Ibid, page 56
[viii] Ibid, page58

[ix] Anonymous

[x] Oswald Chambers, If You Will Ask, Discovery House, 1989, page 1

[xi] Jack R. Taylor, Prayer: Life's Limitless Reach, Broadman Press, 1977, page 12

[xii] Norman Geisler, Christian Apologetics, Baker Book House, 1976, page 362

[xiii] J. I. Packer, Knowing God, Intervarsity Press, 1973, page103
[xiv] Ibid, page 108

[xv] Bobby Eklund & Terry Austin, Partners with God, Convention Press, 1994, page 63
[xvi] Ibid, page 108

[xvii] Ben Gill, The Joy of Giving, 1994, Myriad Communications, Inc., page 1

[xviii] Randy Alcorn, Money Possessions and Eternity, Tyndale Momentum, 2003, page 183

END NOTES

[xix] David Green, Giving It All Away, Harper Collins Publishers, 2017, page 79

[xx] Ibid, page 92

[xxi] Wikipedia "Howard Hendricks"

[xxii] Walter Ian Thomas, The Mystery of Godliness, CLC Publications, 2015, page 10

[xxiii] W. Oscar Thompson, Concentric Circles of Concern, Broadman Publishers, 1999, page 75

[xxiv] Pete Ochs, A High Impact Life, Enterprise Stewardship, 2019, page Introduction II

Contact the Arthur

George C. Hale

geochale@aol.com